THE EXBURY JUNKERS
A WORLD WAR II MYSTERY

First edition, published in 2004 by

Woodfield Publishing
Woodfield House, Babsham Lane, Bognor Regis
West Sussex PO21 5EL, England
www.woodfieldpublishing.com

ISBN 1-903953-60-X

Front cover photograph: EN Archive.

The Exbury Junkers

A WORLD WAR II MYSTERY

JOHN STANLEY

Woodfield

In memory of the seven

Hans Czipin
Hans Ehrhardt
Johann Krause
Robert Schultes
Leonhard Schwingenstein
Edgar Vester
Eitel Wysotzki

~ CONTENTS ~

FOREWORD by Edmund de Rothschild xi
INTRODUCTION The Quest Begins xiii
CHAPTER 1 Early Morning Intruder 1
CHAPTER 2 Crash and Aftermath 15
CHAPTER 3 Investigation and Speculation 32
CHAPTER 4 The Mystery of the Seven Men 36
CHAPTER 5 The Luftwaffe Perspective 48
CHAPTER 6 Into the Hornets' Nest 58
CHAPTER 7 The Blurring of Fiction and Fact 66
CHAPTER 8 Unravelling the Threads 74
CHAPTER 9 A Few Loose Ends 86
CHAPTER 10 Reflections 91
NOTES 108
ACKNOWLEDGEMENTS 114
LIST OF ILLUSTRATIONS 119
BIBLIOGRAPHY 122
INDEX 124

'I came on an enigma of this curious war,
in a small country lane with fields on either side,
very near the sea.'

(Lt-Cdr Nevil Shute Norway, Ministry of Information article, 1944)

FOREWORD

by Edmund de Rothschild

I would like to pay tribute to John Stanley, who has so painstakingly researched an event which occurred in April 1944, when a Junkers 188 with more than its normal complement of personnel was shot down over the park in front of Exbury House, which had been commandeered by the Royal Navy as the stone frigate HMS Mastodon; a crash which resulted in the death of seven young men. Nevil Shute's book *Requiem for a Wren* outlines the significance of the Exbury area and the Beaulieu river at that time. There was a deep mystery about what role, if any, the Junkers was undertaking, given the view that its crew would have had of the craft massed in the Solent, the Beaulieu river and other adjacent areas, several weeks before D-Day and the Normandy landings.

The reader will find this book absorbing with its unanswered questions. I am the owner of Exbury House, but was not a witness to the incident itself as I was a gunner in action in Italy at the Battle of Cassino at the time. Nevertheless, I have learnt a great deal about the truth behind this wartime enigma from what John Stanley has so conscientiously recorded.

Edmund de Rothschild CBE TD

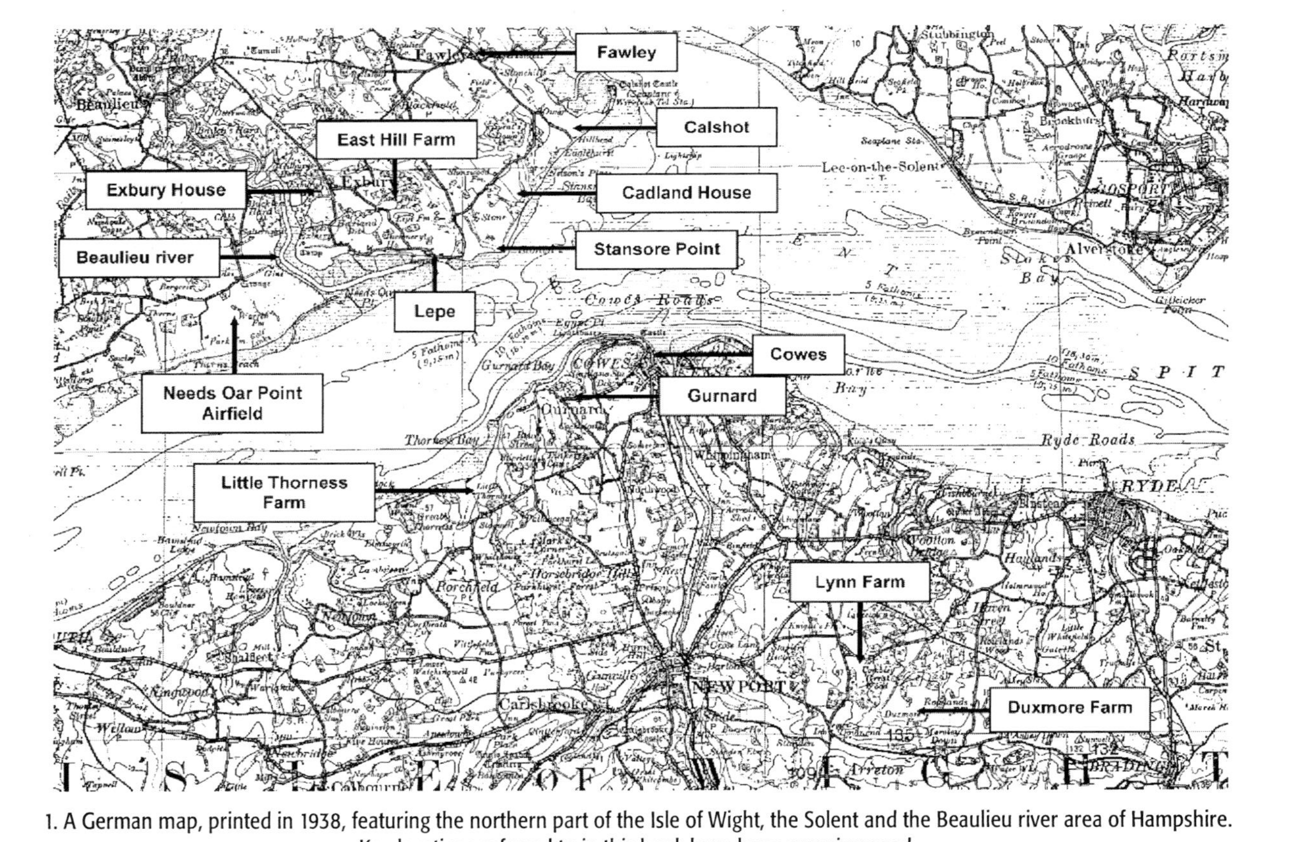

1. A German map, printed in 1938, featuring the northern part of the Isle of Wight, the Solent and the Beaulieu river area of Hampshire. Key locations referred to in this book have been superimposed.

INTRODUCTION

The Quest Begins

This story began for me in July 1996 during a family holiday on the Isle of Wight. Little did I know, as I wandered round an exhibition commemorating the island's experiences of World War II, accompanied by my wife and two young children who were none too keen to be there, that I was about to embark on a quest which was to occupy much of my spare time over the following six years.

One of the exhibits instantly caught my attention. This was a display featuring the recollections of the late Jock Leal, who had served with the Royal Observer Corps on the Isle of Wight during the last war. He had been on duty at an observer post near Newport when a lone German bomber, a Junkers Ju 188, had emerged from the clouds early on the morning of 18 April 1944. L/Observer Leal had recorded the enemy aircraft's every move, and witnessed its inevitable demise on the Hampshire mainland. In documenting this wartime incident, he had made particular reference to the strange behaviour of the German plane – the fact that it had circled low over the Isle of Wight and fired red Very lights each time that it was attacked, and the apparent lack of any return fire or evasive action. He had also drawn attention to the fact that this bomber had been found to be carrying more than its normal complement of men. From that moment on, I was well and truly hooked!

In the following weeks, the more I discovered about the mysterious circumstances surrounding this incident, and the considerable speculation to which it has given rise over the years, the more I resolved to discover exactly what had caused the Junkers to make its ill-fated flight to southern England shortly before D-Day. Surely, it could have been no coincidence that the Ju 188 had loitered over an area where much of the Allied invasion force was being assembled?

As I managed to find more eyewitnesses to the events of 18 April 1944, and delved into official records, I became increasingly fascinated by the human aspects of this story. It became imperative for me to find out something about the seven men who had been travelling on board the Junkers that morning, in order to try to make some sense of this mysterious affair. Of all those who have kindly assisted me with my research (listed in the Acknowledgements), I have been particularly indebted to the relatives of four of the seven men who lost their lives on that April morning. In each case, they have been happy to correspond with me, and have allowed me to reproduce photographs and personal details of the men in this book. I have been deeply touched by their trust. As for those relatives who were unwilling to communicate with me, despite my disappointment, I respect their wish for privacy.

It is important to bear in mind that this curious incident happened sixty years ago now. I am not at all surprised to have come across one or two minor discrepancies amongst the recollections which I have been privileged to hear, and I hope that the many eyewitnesses who have taken the trouble to contact me will forgive me for suggesting that memory can sometimes play tricks with the passing of the years. Nevertheless, I am satisfied that the version of events presented in this book is as accurate as it possibly could be after all this time. In describing what happened on 18 April 1944, I have told much of the story through the eyes of those people who actually saw what happened. In some cases, these accounts are particularly vivid; a number of the eyewitnesses have commented that what they saw at Exbury on that bright spring morning is permanently etched in their memory.

Where appropriate, I have supplemented the eyewitness accounts with details from British and German official records. I have also provided some background information from several expert sources, in order for an understanding to be gained of the historical context in which this wartime incident occurred.

The writer Nevil Shute was among those who were greatly fascinated by the Junkers incident. His novel *Requiem for a Wren*, published in 1955, has a fictional account of the shooting down of the Ju 188 at Exbury as its centrepiece. Whilst some aspects of the incident are described accurately in the novel, others are pure invention. This blurring of fiction and fact has undoubtedly helped to create some of the myths surrounding the events of 18 April 1944. Indeed, in more than one case, I have found that the recollections of an eyewitness have, in some way, been influenced by Shute's fictional account.

During the course of my research I have encountered the peripheral, but lively, debate as to whether the spit of land at the entrance to the Beaulieu river should be called Needs Oar Point or Needs Ore Point. The Advanced Landing Ground, established just to the west of this location in the run-up to D-Day, was named Needs Oar Point. However, the spelling Ore appears both on historical charts and modern Ordnance Survey maps. For consistency, given that this book is concerned with events during the last war, I have used the Oar spelling throughout. I trust that those readers who have strong views on this subject will bear with me.

As my investigations have progressed, it has become increasingly clear that I would have to be satisfied with degrees of probability rather than the absolute certainty to which I had originally aspired. As you will find, whilst it is possible to arrive at a reason for the lone German bomber's flight into the heart of the Allied D-Day preparations, there remain several unanswered questions which will surely serve to keep the mystery alive.

Finally, I should point out that I do not profess to be a Luftwaffe expert or to have any specialist knowledge of aviation. The assessments I have made about the Exbury Junkers incident have been based purely on an analysis of the available information. Readers will undoubtedly form their own opinions about this curious wartime tale.

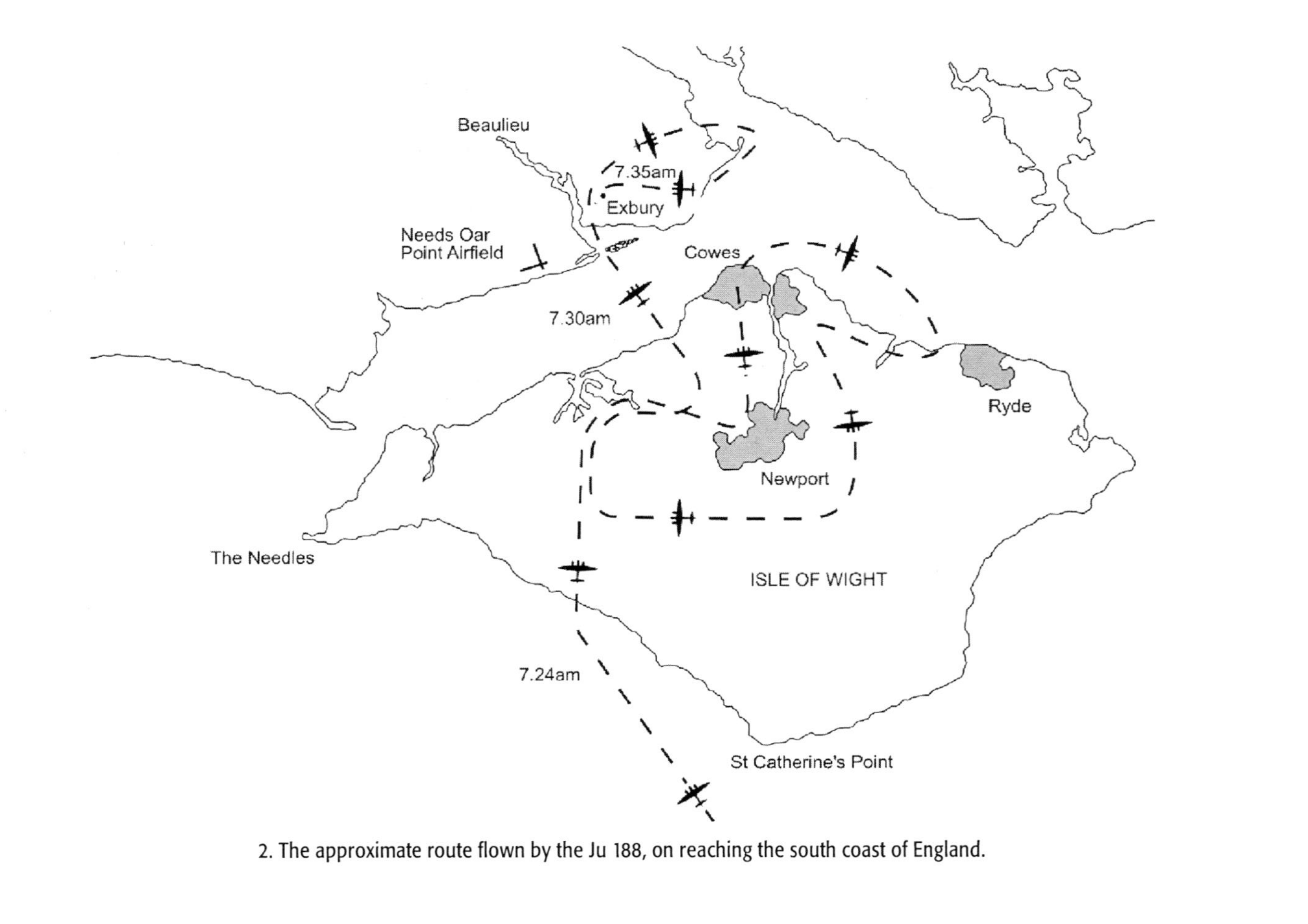

2. The approximate route flown by the Ju 188, on reaching the south coast of England.

CHAPTER 1

Early Morning Intruder

There was a weather front lying close to Bourges in central France at daybreak on Tuesday 18 April 1944. At nearby Avord airfield a German bomber, a Junkers Ju 188, lumbered down the runway in steady rain and disappeared into the gloom.[1]

3. A Ju 188 bomber

At 7.03am, the Junkers was detected by British radar. By this time it was 15 miles west of Le Havre and flying in a north-westerly direction towards England, at a height of 600ft.[2] As the plane flew out over the English Channel, weather conditions had significantly improved. The rain had died out, the cloud was much higher, and visibility had greatly increased.[3] The German bomber continued steadily on the same north-westerly heading towards the Isle of Wight. By the time it was half-way between Le Havre and St Catherine's Point, on the southern tip of the Isle of Wight, it had climbed to around 4,000ft.[4]

It had been a quiet night for the Royal Observer Corps on the Isle of Wight, with no enemy air activity detected. However, at 7.24am, observer posts received the plot of a hostile aircraft approaching the island. The ROC alarm and air raid sirens were sounded immediately.[5]

Meanwhile, there had been a most peculiar development at Royal Observer Corps 3 Group HQ in Winchester. Phyllis Lehan was a 'teller' in the Operations Room. Her job was to read aircraft plots from the table over the telephone to fighter stations of 11 Group. She was just coming to the end of her night shift as the lone German bomber was nearing the coast of southern England. In advance of the enemy aircraft appearing on the plotting board, information had been received on the top deck of the Operations Room that the Junkers was approaching, and that:

> *It would be flying across the Isle of Wight, and no offensive action would be taken.*

4. A Royal Observer Corps crew gathers round the plotting table in the Operations Room at 3 Group HQ in Winchester.

Phyllis Lehan was astonished at hearing this news, but assumed that somebody very important must have been on board the plane. She knew better than to ask any questions.

The Junkers reached the south coast of the Isle of Wight, mid-way between St Catherine's Point and the Needles. In its first significant change of direction since leaving its base, the German bomber turned due north and flew directly over the island. At this point the pilot brought the plane down out of the clouds to about 1,000ft, and the Royal Observer Corps gained their first sighting of the early morning intruder.[6] On approaching the north coast of the island, in the Newtown area, the Ju 188 turned sharply eastwards. As it did so, L/Observer Jock Leal, who was watching the bomber from the observer post at Mount Joy near Newport, saw a red Very light being fired from the German plane. This was to be the first of a number of red signalling flares which were seen to emanate from the cockpit of the Junkers.[7]

5. Jock Leal (standing, right) with fellow members of the Royal Observer Corps outside 3/JIG 1 Post at Mount Joy, on the Isle of Wight.

Ten-year-old Peter Montgomery lived on the north-western outskirts of Newport. He was awoken by the sounding of the air raid siren not long after dawn. As he looked out the window, he immediately saw a twin-engined bomber flying slowly towards him from the direction of Parkhurst forest.

> *The plane was very low, and anti-aircraft guns, probably the two Bofors on the north-west side of the town, were firing at it.*

Peter could also see two small lights twinkling side-by-side in the nose of the bomber. He lost sight of the aircraft after about 30 seconds.

Before reaching the river Medina, the Junkers turned sharply to port and flew almost due north towards West Cowes. According to several eyewitnesses, the German bomber circled low over Somerton Aerodrome at Cowes, almost as if it had been looking to land. This was the only airfield on the Isle of Wight which had been kept open during the war.[8] The enemy plane then turned away from West Cowes and flew a short distance out into the Solent and eastwards past East Cowes. As it did so, it attracted the attention of a number of ships which were anchored in the stretch of water known as Cowes Roads. James Carroll was 18 years old and in the Merchant Navy. He was serving on the Princess Margaret, a ship carrying Royal Marine Commandos who were training for D-Day. The Junkers passed directly overhead James's ship, and several of the vessels around him began firing at the enemy plane.

The German bomber next wheeled round to starboard and crossed the Isle of Wight's northern coast again, between East Cowes and Ryde. It proceeded to fly a meandering clockwise circuit over the northern part of the island, and came under attack from several anti-aircraft batteries.

George Shave was travelling from Sandown to East Cowes on a works bus as usual that morning. When they had reached a point to the east of Newport, he and his workmates caught sight of the German bomber to the right and ahead of them. It was flying slowly and fairly low.

> *As the Junkers turned southwards towards us we left the bus for a roadside ditch. We were close enough to see the cross on the side of the fuselage as it passed by. We watched its flight for about two minutes until it turned away north-westwards.*

John Meredith was also watching the Ju 188 at the same moment. He was at Duxmore Farm on the Isle of Wight. He had been alerted to the presence of the German bomber by the sound of massive anti-aircraft fire and the smoke from the exploding shells. He believed that it was being fired on by a Polish destroyer moored at East Cowes. When John caught sight of the Junkers it was heading southwards. It was flying in a straight line and under control.

> *As the bomber drew nearer it pulled up. Its pointed wingtips were clearly visible, and it was easily identifiable as a Ju 188. The black crosses on the fuselage could clearly be seen. One of the lads working at Duxmore Farm was in the Home Guard. He had an automatic rifle. On seeing the German plane he fetched his gun and balanced it on my shoulder, ready to do battle, but his efforts were in vain.*

6. Several eyewitnesses recognised the Ju 188 on account of its pointed wingtips.

The Junkers was about to fly directly over the anti-aircraft battery at Lynn Farm, just to the north-west of Duxmore. Around a dozen guns were tracking its path as it approached. They fired the usual ranging shot, and this appeared to hit the aircraft dead centre. The bomber immediately reared up, then turned away to the west, gradually losing height. Although it seemed to have been hit, the Ju 188 still seemed perfectly under control.

Miraculously, the Junkers had somehow managed to withstand the barrage of anti-aircraft fire, which had been directed at it thus far. The fact that it was flying so low must surely have counted in its favour but, even so, its continued survival caused astonishment among those who were observing its curious flight.

The Royal Observer Corps post at Mount Joy next reported the intruder flying westwards just to the south of Newport. It continued its clockwise circuit over the northern part of the Isle of Wight, turning northwards then eastwards. According to the ROC, red Very lights were fired from the Junkers each time that it changed direction.[9] The enemy plane finally broke off its circuit to head in a north-westerly direction towards the Solent.

William Fuller and his brother had just left their house in Gurnard, on the north-west coast, on their way to catch the ferry to East Cowes for work, which started at 7.45am. The German bomber suddenly came into view; it was flying level, straight and under control. They watched it fly out over the Solent.

Meanwhile, John Hayward was working on nearby Little Thorness Farm when the Junkers appeared at about 7.30am. It was flying well below the clouds. From its black underside, it was initially difficult to tell whether this was a German or an RAF bomber. A twin-barrelled Vickers anti-aircraft gun was positioned in a field on the farm, right next to a hedge which had been cut away to allow the gun to fire westwards. As it quickly became apparent that this was indeed an enemy aircraft, the corporal in charge ran to the Vickers gun and started firing. This was the first time that the gun had been used in anger. John Hayward saw tracer bullets going into the belly of the Junkers, but it remained under control and did not alter its north-westerly course. John also saw red Very lights being fired from the bomber.

> *They were fired in pairs three or four times. They quickly burned out and fell to earth.*

The Ju 188 crossed the island's coastline over Thorness Bay. It had defied all attempts to shoot it down.

It was a fine spring morning on the Hampshire coast. A weather report issued by an observer at Lee-on-Solent gave the following conditions at 6am: broken cloud at 1,500ft, dry but hazy, visibility four miles and a light north-easterly wind.[10]

As the lone German bomber steadily made its way across the Solent, coincidentally a number of RAF fighter-bombers were close at hand. F/Lt Vernon Sanders was leading a section of four Hawker Typhoons from 266 (Rhodesia) Squadron back to their base at Needs Oar Point, at the approach to the Beaulieu river. They had been taking part in an activity codenamed *Exercise Smash*.[11]

The Junkers crossed the Hampshire coast over the approach to the Beaulieu river, close to the airfield at Needs Oar Point. Mac McMurdon, a Typhoon pilot with 266 Squadron, was relaxing in the sunshine with several other pilots outside their tents when they were taken by surprise by the spectre of the low-flying German bomber.

> *We at the tents heard ack-ack guns firing and the air raid sirens were screaming. All of sudden the Junkers flew over us at very low level (tree-top height). It was firing Very cartridges. We saw the German black crosses on the plane quite clearly.*

The anti-aircraft fire, which Mac McMurdon could hear, was coming from the Bofors gun which was positioned on the Lower Exbury marshes, guarding the entrance to the Beaulieu river.

Just after 7.30am, the Ju 188 passed almost directly over Exbury House, which had been commandeered as the naval base HMS Mastodon. The base was a hive of activity at this time, just seven weeks before D-Day. Not only was it involved generally in the planning for the Allied invasion of France, but it was also responsible specifically for the servicing of the fleet of landing craft which had been assembled in the Beaulieu river, and it had become a temporary camp and training centre for a variety of specialised naval units; a veritable hornets' nest.

Seventeen-year-old Sam Mundy was a despatch rider at HMS Mastodon. He was quartered in one of the Nissen huts which had been constructed in a spinney to the east side of Exbury House, south of the greenhouse gardens. As he was returning to his hut after having a wash, he was astonished to see a German plane suddenly appearing from behind the house, flying in a north-easterly direction. It cleared the nearby water tower by a matter of feet and quickly disappeared from view.

> *I had a hard job convincing those still in bed that I had just seen a German bomber.*

7. Sam Mundy (centre)

From Exbury the Junkers flew eastwards. As it reached the Calshot area, at the approach to Southampton Water, it circled round and flew directly over the RAF base there. Ron Woolhead had been stationed at RAF Calshot since 1943. He was working with a ferry crew which took high speed launches from the local boatyards to different dockyards all over the country. He had just sat down to breakfast that morning when the German bomber thundered directly over the dining room. No warning had been given, and everyone had been taken completely by surprise by this low-flying intruder.

8. The water tower on the Exbury estate, which the Junkers just cleared as it flew directly over the naval base HMS Mastodon.

As the bomber began to turn westwards, the four Typhoons of 266 Squadron were approaching Needs Oar Point airfield, having completed their part in *Exercise Smash*. They had just flown over the southeast-northwest runway in line astern ready to land when F/Lt Sanders spotted a line of heavy anti-aircraft shell bursts in front of him, at a height of about 1,500ft. The bursts were above, behind and slightly to starboard of an aircraft which he immediately believed to be a Ju 188. The German bomber was flying from east to west, at about 1,000ft. Sanders and F/Sgt Donovan Dodd immediately peeled off to investigate. According to Sanders's subsequent combat report:

> *It turned to port, and I turned inside it, at a height of about 500ft. Closing in, I confirmed that the bomber was a Ju 188, and clearly recognised its markings.*

At this point Sanders reported that he had experienced slight return fire from the German plane.[12]

Two young boys saw the Typhoons begin their attack on the Junkers. Maldwin Drummond and his brother were in their bedroom at Cadland House, near the coast, just down from Calshot. Their attention was suddenly attracted by the noise of engines above the house and a spatter of machine-gun fire.

> *As we looked out we saw at least two Typhoons pursuing a twin-engined bomber, which was making from east to west. I seem to remember the bomber firing red Very lights.*

The boys lost sight of the German plane as it flew westwards towards Exbury. It looked as if it was coming down, since there was some smoke and parts were falling from it, although it was still apparently flying under control. Eager to find out what had happened to the bomber, Maldwin's father and the two children climbed into their Ford shooting-brake and set off for Exbury.

The Junkers headed back towards Exbury with the two Typhoons, piloted by Sanders and Dodd, in hot pursuit. Sanders later reported that he opened fire from about 200yds, with slight deflection, from behind on the port side.

> *I observed strikes on the cockpit and the port wing root, and saw flames and smoke coming from this area.*[13]

9. An RAF Hawker Typhoon Mk 1B, similar to those of 266 Squadron which pounced on the lone Junkers.

After firing only 100 rounds, Sanders's guns jammed, or he was unable to get into the right position to finish off the German plane. Don Dodd then took over and raked the Junkers extensively with cannon-fire.

The stricken bomber was spotted by Honor Johnston as it continued its flight westwards towards Exbury. She lived at nearby East Hill Farm, and had been alerted to the presence of the enemy plane by the sound of gunfire coming from the anti-aircraft site at Lepe Farm, just a mile or so to the south.

Meanwhile, a group of Land Girls had just arrived for work in a field to the east of Exbury village. Included in their number were Marjorie Pinnock, Nancy Jones and Bunty Cooper. The girls, who all came originally from Nottingham, had travelled to Exbury that morning from Beaulieu, where they were accommodated in a hostel. Under the supervision of Mr Vardy, the owner of the threshing set, the Land Girls were just about to start threshing the corn when the German bomber appeared from the east without any warning whatsoever. It was just above tree-top height, and its frighteningly huge, black underside momentarily blocked out the sunlight. The two RAF fighters pursuing the bomber were positioned above and behind it.

> *The Typhoons were firing at the bomber and bullets were flying everywhere. Mr Vardy told us to take cover underneath the threshing set. The gunfire lasted for no more than five seconds. There was no sign of the German plane returning fire. The bomber was losing height as it disappeared over Exbury, and we were certain that it was about to crash.*

10. The Land Army Girls stared in excitement as the low-flying German bomber made its sudden, dramatic appearance. However, they soon had to take cover, as shells from the Typhoons' cannon-fire were flying everywhere.

Leopold de Rothschild and his elder sister, Rosemary, were staying at their mother's house, Marise Cottage, in Exbury village, opposite the main drive to Exbury House. They had been awoken that morning by the sound of loud gunfire. Looking out of the bedroom windows, which faced east, they saw the Junkers flying low and very close to the house. The two Typhoons were approximately 200-300ft behind it. The three aircraft then turned a complete circle and returned one or two minutes later. At least one of the Typhoons was firing at the bomber, but there was no sign of any return fire. The anti-aircraft guns at Lepe Farm could also be heard. As the Junkers appeared for a second time, black smoke could be seen, possibly coming from its port engine.

Alan Fields, 16 at the time, was standing by the Exbury village stores when he heard the noise of engines and gunfire. He then watched in disbelief as the Junkers flew very low over the village, pursued by the two Typhoons.

> *They fanned the German plane with cannon-fire from close range. As this was happening, I noticed something white hanging out of the port-side cockpit window – possibly clothing or a parachute. It was all over in seconds but it was clear that the bomber was going to crash.*

Sylvia Johnston, an evacuee from Southampton, was living in a cottage close to the village stores, on the Lower Exbury road, with her mother, aunt, sister, two brothers and three cousins. On hearing the sound of the anti-aircraft fire from the battery at Lepe, they had rushed outside, and were just in time to see the German bomber flying so low that it narrowly avoided hitting the roof of the cottage. As it passed overhead, smoke was trailing behind it. The plane was so close that they could actually see a face looking out of the cockpit. It was obvious to them that the bomber was about to crash, and so they all ran down the Lower Exbury road towards the place where they thought it was coming down.

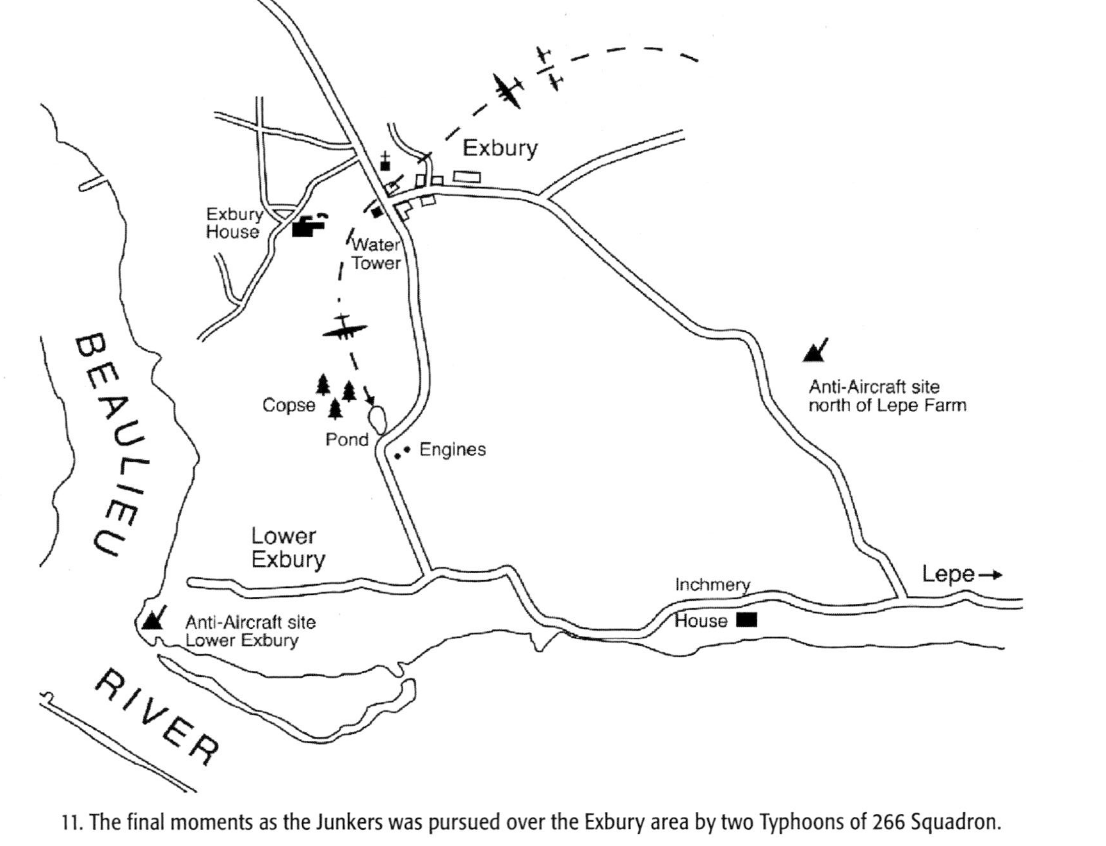

11. The final moments as the Junkers was pursued over the Exbury area by two Typhoons of 266 Squadron.

CHAPTER 2

Crash and Aftermath

Many servicemen at HMS Mastodon witnessed the final moments as the Junkers descended over the Exbury estate. Sam Mundy, the despatch rider, was still trying to convince his colleagues in one of the Nissen huts that he had seen a German bomber when it returned, from the direction of the water tower over which it had disappeared minutes earlier. Sam had heard two bursts of gunfire before it re-appeared.

Harry Smelt was a member of the HMS Mastodon fire-crew. He was a Royal Navy stoker and, along with three other men of the same rank, had been posted to Exbury in 1943, after completing a fire-fighting course at HMS Vernon in Portsmouth. Harry had just been carrying out the daily test of the fire-pump by the potting shed, close to Exbury House, when the Junkers and its two assailants appeared overhead. Some people took cover at the sound of the Typhoons' cannon-fire, and the bomber's engines were spluttering and leaving a trail of smoke.

12. RN stoker Harry Smelt

Some 80 men from Assault Group 1, Force J, were assembled on the parade-ground next to Exbury House as there suddenly came the noise of low-flying aircraft and the Junkers appeared from behind the house, with the two Typhoons on its tail.[1] Meanwhile, HMS Mastodon's dental surgeon, Surgeon Lt (D), RNVR, Richard Stephens, had just returned to his room on the first floor of Exbury House when he heard the loud rattle of gunfire. Looking out of his window over the colonnade, he suddenly caught sight of the German bomber flying very low past the house in a southerly direction and descending at a shallow angle.

George James, a telegraphist serving with Combined Operations Bombardment Unit, was billeted in one of the Nissen huts. He was awoken by a loud rushing noise, dressed hurriedly and emerged into the sunlight just in time to see the action.

13. Marine John Lambourne

Bullets were flying everywhere; some rebounded off the roofs of the Nissen huts.

At the same moment, a number of Marines and naval ratings from Combined Operations Bombardment Unit were just returning from breakfast. They could not believe their eyes as they looked up through the trees close to Exbury House and saw a V-formation of low-flying aircraft, with two Typhoons firing at the German bomber from close range. Included in this group was 19-year-old John Lambourne, a Marine serving with Landing Craft Support. He was at Mastodon with a number of other Marines undergoing intensive training in signals, since it had been decided that, on D-Day, landing craft should be able to maintain contact with their parent ship.

Having initially taken cover at the sound of gunfire, John looked up through the trees to see the enormous shape of the bomber passing slowly overhead. It was so close and low that he could clearly make out the pilot and co-pilot in the front of the cockpit. His first thought was that the German plane was a lone hit-and-run raider, and that it was strafing the camp. However, this impression quickly changed when John spotted a Typhoon climbing sharply as the Junkers descended towards the ground.

As John watched the German plane come down, apparently under control, he was convinced that it was going to land in the field to the south of Exbury House, and he set off after it in keen anticipation of taking its crew prisoner.

Meanwhile, 17-year-old Arthur Sibley was trying to get his tractor to start. He had been working in a field on the south side of the Lower Exbury road, and was about to go to breakfast, when he heard the distant sound of gunfire. Moments later, he suddenly became aware of the German bomber heading straight towards him from the village side of Exbury House.

> *I saw the Typhoons on either side of the Junkers, and could clearly make out their cannon-fire. I dived for cover.*

From a distance, several servicemen at HMS Mastodon saw the Junkers crash-land in the field south of Exbury House, which was a part of the estate known locally as 'The Park'. The plane skidded along the ground for a short distance before coming to a sudden, violent halt on encountering a shallow pond, which lay in a patch of boggy ground in the far corner of the field. As it crashed into the pond, its two engines broke away from the wings. There was an explosion, and a fire broke out in the cockpit area, which quickly engulfed the rest of the fuselage. As F/Lt Vernon Sanders flew over the crashed Junkers, he *saw it burning on the ground with a heavy column of smoke rising from it.*[2] One of the Typhoons performed a victory-roll as it flew above the burning wreckage.

Leading Seaman Reg 'Tug' Wilson had a particularly close shave. He was in charge of the guard on the Exbury estate and at nearby Lepe House. He had been to visit his wife at Holbury, an adjacent village, the previous night, because she had just given birth to a baby girl. Having checked the guard at Lepe House, Reg was cycling back along the lane towards the camp at Exbury when he heard the sound of anti-aircraft fire. Suddenly, he caught sight of the German bomber coming straight towards him from the direction of Exbury House. He *had to bike like hell to get out of the way* as the Junkers crashed into the pond close to the road, and its two engines came rolling through the hedge *like two huge balls of twisted metal.*

I consider myself very lucky. If I had been five seconds later, I would have been run down by one of those engines. There was nowhere to go, or even time to think of it.

14. Leading Seaman Reg 'Tug' Wilson pictured with his wife and baby daughter, shortly after the Junkers crash. Reg had narrowly avoided the engines of the German bomber as he cycled along the lane to Exbury.

L/Observer Jock Leal, who had been following the Ju 188's every move from an observer post on the Isle of Wight, later recorded:

All this time, it had been dropping red flares. Its speed never exceeded 250mph. It never flew higher than 1,000ft. It passed over many military objectives without dropping a bomb or firing a gun. Nor did a single gun reply when the Typhoons screamed up....and poured fire into this strange intruder. We watched in amazement as the Junkers Ju 188 crashed in a mass of flames.[3]

The time was approximately 7.35am.

Marine John Lambourne had already set off for the field, fully expecting to take the German crew prisoner. Many naval ratings also ran from the area of the Nissen huts and climbed through the hedge and over the barbed wire which marked the perimeter of HMS Mastodon. Neil Gregory, and his comrades in C Troop, Combined Operations Bombardment Unit, ignored a shouted warning from a superior that this action amounted to *breaking ship* and, as such, was a serious offence.

Sam Mundy, the despatch rider, had also set off for the crash site:

> *I saw others running in the direction of a spinney. By this time quite a few were heading towards the crash. As we neared the plane, someone shouted, 'Get down!' A Royal Marine Commando near me shouted that they (the German crew) were going to shoot at us.*

The gunner's turret on the Ju 188 appeared to be turning, and it was thought that the gunner was going to shoot. However, it transpired that, on impact, the turret had somehow been jammed in the revolving position. The gunner himself was dead.

Those arriving at the corner of the field where the Junkers had met its end found a scene of total devastation. The plane was badly broken up, wreckage was strewn across a wide area, and the fuselage had quickly burnt out. First on the scene were Marine John Lambourne, and Neil Gregory and George James from Combined Operations Bombardment Unit. As John reached the wrecked bomber, he immediately noticed two men lying on their backs on the green banking beneath the hedge, which lined the narrow road to Lower Exbury. They had obviously been thrown forwards out of the cockpit. Both men were wearing a blue-grey Luftwaffe tunic and a brown flying helmet. The first man he approached seemed very young, with fair hair and bright blue eyes. He had a glazed expression and was obviously concussed but showed no external injuries. On loosening the young man's collar, John

15. Neil Gregory, C Troop, Combined Operations Bombardment Unit

suddenly heard him start to mumble a few words in German. At this point he checked with another serviceman, who was tending the second casualty lying under the hedge. It seemed that this young man was also still alive, but only just. It was astonishing that there were no visible signs of injury to either man nor damage to their clothing despite the distance they had been thrown.

Having combed the site, George James found five bodies in all. In addition to the two men lying under the hedge, he found another man lying on his back in the middle of the road beyond the hedge. He was still alive, and again had no visible injuries, other than what seemed like a gravel-rash on his face. However, he died almost immediately in George's arms. A fourth man was found on the side of the ditch lining the road. George went to lift him up, but he was very badly injured and evidently beyond help. The fifth man whom George came across was lying in the pond to the rear of the wreckage. He was clearly dead. George also climbed inside the remains of the plane. On hearing the sound of hissing, which he assumed to be oxygen bottles, it suddenly occurred to him that there could be unexploded bombs on board, so he beat a hasty retreat.

Neil Gregory also came across the young man lying in the pond to the rear of the wreckage. He had the blast effect all over his face and body. As Neil made his way towards the plane there were shouts of alarm that ammunition was exploding. He moved on to the next casualty, one of the men lying next to the hedge. George James was already tending to the man, and it was obvious that he had no chance of surviving.

Meanwhile, back in the Royal Observer Corps Operations Room in Winchester, the news had been received that the German bomber had been shot down. Phyllis Lehan, the 'teller' who had earlier been privy to the information that no offensive action was going to be taken against the incoming Junkers, thought to herself that *someone will be in trouble.*

As the search continued for signs of life among the carnage at the crash site, a surprising fact began to emerge. There had been an unusually large number of men on board this aircraft. The normal crew complement for a bomber of this type was thought to be four, and yet as many as seven bodies had been found; four of the men had been hurled forwards out of the cockpit, whilst a further three, who displayed terrible injuries, were found in or close to the wreckage in the pond. The camp's dentist, Surgeon Lt (D) Richard Stephens, its medical officer and Sick Berth CPO Albert Daniels, who had all hurried to the scene, were treating the survivors as best they could. At one point, George James needed to take some drastic action:

> *As there were civilians, including children, edging their way along the lane, I opened two or three parachutes to cover the bodies.*

This could have led to the impression formed by some eyewitnesses that the men on board the Junkers had tried to use their parachutes, but had baled out too low.

16. HMS Mastodon Transport Section, after D-Day. Sam Mundy is fifth from left (back row).

The medical officer asked Sam Mundy, the despatch rider, to provide some transport to have the survivors taken to the sick bay at HMS Mastodon.

> *As I ran to the Transport Section, I was considering the best way to get a vehicle close to the plane which had crashed into the bog. Then I remembered that the engines of the plane had been torn out of their*

> *mountings, and had rolled across the field, through the hedge, across the road, through a second hedge, and had come to rest some 60ft inside the next field. When I saw one of the drivers, I advised him to take the Lower Exbury road, and to take the casualties through the holes in the hedge made by the engines.*

Richard Stephens, the dentist, gathered from those who had reached the crash site before him that the intention was for those crew members showing some signs of life to be brought over to the sick bay. He ran back to it to prepare for their arrival.

Within minutes, a field ambulance had been taken down the Lower Exbury road and parked next to the hedge where the engines of the Junkers had burst through. The two young men who had been found lying on their backs beneath the hedge were placed on stretchers, which were then passed over the low hedge to the waiting ambulance. These were the only survivors out of the seven men who had been on board the German bomber.

Ian Gordon, a coder with HQ Ships Signals, Assault Group 1, Force J, saw one of the men being carried to the ambulance on a stretcher.

> *He was a fair-haired young lad, wearing a grey uniform. He appeared to be unconscious.*

A Wren Motor Transport driver, who served under Captain Pugsley, commander of Assault Group 1, Force J, had driven two Marine Commandos down the Lower Exbury road to see what had happened. She was told that one of the young crew was still alive, though badly injured, and that he was in the field ambulance standing nearby.

Allan 'Jimmy' Green, who was a Sick Berth Attendant at HMS Mastodon from 1942 to 1946, remembers one of the men being brought to the sick bay, which was on the left hand side of the main drive leading to Exbury House. It was clear that the young man's injuries were so serious that nothing could be done for him.

I remember him being good-looking, with light hair. I have often regretted that I was unable to tell his family that his passing on was peaceful. His image remains with me.

17. Allan 'Jimmy' Green, Sick Berth Attendant at HMS Mastodon from 1942 to 1946.

18. Allan Green (left) pictured with his colleagues outside the sick bay (a Nissen hut just to the left of the main drive, close to Exbury House).

Richard Stephens, the dentist, also looked after one of the men who had been brought to the sick bay. He was deeply unconscious, and all that could be done for him was to keep his airways open and to give him oxygen. He passed away after several hours.

I saw that he had a leather wallet half projecting from his jacket. I pulled it out, took a glance at it, but pushed it back again for investigating staff to deal with. I rather regretted not making a note of the names of his parents or wife or girlfriend, as I could then have contacted them after the end of the war to assure them that this airman would have been rendered instantly unconscious on the impact of the crash and never regained consciousness, and that he did not suffer. Also that we did all we could to save him.

19. Surgeon Lt (D) Richard Stephens, HMS Mastodon's dentist, pictured (left) on the verandah of Exbury House, with his colleagues Second Officer Mary Dudley, Officer-in-Charge of all Wrens at Mastodon, and Lt-Cdr Walter Lord, RNR, the paymaster.

Wren Kathleen Hern was a shorthand typist in the secretariat at nearby Lepe House. That morning she had occasion to attend the sick bay at HMS Mastodon. Having walked into the Nissen hut she was astonished to see a young German airman there. He looked very ill.

> *I thought when I looked at him that he was very like my brother, blond and blue-eyed, and I suddenly felt, 'What are we all fighting for? It seems so futile.' I have often thought that perhaps I was one of the last people he ever saw.*

Meanwhile, back at the crash site the engines of the Ju 188, which had ended up some distance into the field across the road, were being examined by Maurice Barker. He was employed at the Supermarine works in Southampton and his job was to inspect repairs made to RAF planes. At that time, Maurice happened to be staying with his parents, who lived in Exbury village. He had been awoken that morning, like so many others locally, by a short burst of cannon-fire, and had looked out to see the German bomber just clearing the rooftops and trailing a plume of black smoke.

20. Maurice Barker happened to be staying with his parents at Exbury when the German bomber came to grief. Maurice instantly recognised the wrecked plane as a Ju 188 from its unique BMW-801 radial engines. The Spitfire badge on his lapel was worn by all Supermarine employees.

By the time he had reached the crash site, a crowd of servicemen from HMS Mastodon were already gathered there. Maurice saw that the two engines, minus their propellers, had rolled across the road and into the next field. They were being guarded by two sailors. He presented his RAF pass, which authorised him to inspect crashed aircraft, and made his way to the engines. He immediately recognised them as BMW-801 radials, the most advanced of their type when introduced. He knew these to be unique to the Junkers Ju 188.

By this stage in the war, Maurice had examined a number of German aircraft in flying condition, including a Ju 88 which was flown around RAF stations to give the anti-aircraft gunners a close view. This was why he had *no particular interest in viewing the twisted metal of the crashed Junkers, other than its engines.*

Several dozen servicemen from HMS Mastodon were by now assembled at the scene of the wrecked bomber. They were soon joined by members of one of the nearby anti-aircraft crews which had claimed to have hit the Junkers. About an hour after the crash, the site was also visited by a group of Typhoon pilots, who made the short journey from Needs Oar Point airfield in a light truck. Included in their number was at least one of the pilots from 266 Squadron who had intercepted the Ju 188. Mac McMurdon of 266 Squadron and James Kyle of 197 Squadron were also there. By the time they had reached the site, a local policeman had arrived on the scene, and had taken control of the incident. The *burly, red-faced police sergeant* had the onerous duty of working out exactly how many bodies there were in the wreckage of the German bomber. This policeman was observed by several eyewitnesses to pick up a brown, leather, flying boot, only to throw it down in horror when he realised that it contained part of a leg. One of the Typhoon pilots had also had a nasty shock on picking the same flying boot out of the pond.[4]

In amongst the wreckage, items of the crew's personal belongings were scattered about, including what looked like overnight bags. Some French coins were also found. Small pieces of the aircraft were claimed as souvenirs by a number of the Navy servicemen who had attended the crash scene, and some even went away with live ammunition. In several cases, items were taken from the men who had perished in the crash; these included weapons and ammunition, a watch and a belt. A sailor also took an Iron Cross medal from one of the men. Some of these souvenirs were initially hidden down rabbit holes in the nearby copse, or secreted under clothing. News of this activity must have travelled fast for a thorough search of the quarters at HMS Mastodon was ordered when the men had returned to the camp.

Those civilians whose curiosity had drawn them to the crash site found that they were relatively free to wander around the field. David Butler was 11 years old at the time, and he lived a short distance from Exbury. He had heard the sound of the Typhoons' cannon-fire while lying in bed.

News of the demise of the German bomber soon spread, and so he and his friend had set off on their bicycles to visit the site.

> *The main fuselage (riddled with cannon-shell holes) looked reasonably intact, but debris and live ammunition were scattered around the site. It now seems peculiar but, at the time, the public were only prohibited from the immediate fuselage area. Otherwise, we were free to inspect the wreckage and look for souvenirs.*

21. The Land Army Girls went to see the wrecked bomber during their mid-morning break. Nancy Jones (standing third from left) found a lamp containing a card from a German florist's shop.

Several of the Land Army Girls, who had been working in a field just to the east of Exbury village when the Junkers had flown overhead, went to view the crashed bomber during their mid-morning break. In the field, amongst the debris, Nancy Jones found a lamp. When she opened up the back of it, she found an envelope propped up against the battery. The envelope contained a card from a florist's shop in Germany. She did not have the time to study it more closely before it was taken from her by an intelligence officer, who had arrived to carry out a thorough technical inspection of the crashed aircraft, or what was left of it. In the course of this inspection, a number of papers which had been found scattered around the field were gathered up for later examination.

Phyllis Hellier, a WAAF ambulance driver assigned to the Motor Transport Office at RAF Calshot, was detailed to attend the site of the crashed German bomber at Exbury. She took with her an RAF officer who was to be in charge of the removal of the bodies. As she reached the crash site, she turned off the Lower Exbury road down a track and into a small enclosure where soldiers were on guard. This was in the copse close to the spot where the bomber had come to grief. Phyllis was told which way to face the ambulance, and instructed not to leave the cab. Several bodies were then loaded on board. While she was waiting in her cab, a soldier gave her an insignia which had been torn from one of the German uniforms.

22/23. Phyllis Hellier was a WAAF ambulance driver at RAF Calshot. The ambulance which she drove to Exbury to collect the bodies of several of those killed in the Junkers crash was a Morris 14, similar to the one pictured above.

As she set off back down the narrow track, Phyllis Hellier met an open-topped lorry coming in the other direction. She stopped, thinking that the driver would back up and give way to the ambulance, but instead he tried to get past. The lorry struck the canvas and struts of the ambulance's roof causing it to collapse. While the RAF officer and the lorry driver were filling in her form 446, which she had to carry for such eventualities, Phyllis went round the back of the ambulance to inspect the damage. She looked in at the bodies; there were four men, dressed in blue-grey Luftwaffe uniforms, and they had been wrapped in blankets. Once the paperwork had been completed, she took the bodies back to the mortuary at RAF Calshot, without further incident. It appears that the remains of the other three men killed in the Junkers crash were transported to Calshot in an RAF lorry with a canvas roof. The role of the open-topped tipper truck, which had collided with the ambulance is unclear. Several eyewitnesses at the crash site had believed that it was this vehicle which was used to remove the remains of several of the bodies. The fact that an open-topped truck was later seen to off-load its contents at Needs Oar Point airfield makes this even more puzzling. The most likely explanation is, however, that the truck had been sent to the crash site to remove, not bodies, but parts of the wrecked German plane.

24. The Luftwaffe badge which was plucked from the uniform of one of the men killed in the German bomber crash and presented to ambulance driver Phyllis Hellier.

Curiously, the German bomber was not the only aircraft to crash near Exbury that day. A Taylorcraft Auster Mk 4, a light aircraft used by the RAF for observation in support of ground troops and artillery, came down in a field just to the south-east of Exbury village that afternoon. Having earlier witnessed the Junkers being forced down by the RAF Typhoons, and the gruesome carnage at the crash site, the Land Girls from Nottingham spent their lunchtime chatting to the British pilot of the light aircraft, which had landed in a field across the road from where they had been threshing. The man, *jolly, quite young and in civilian clothing*, had been sitting on the grass making notes. He had told the girls that his flimsy aircraft was an *observer plane.* Tragically, after lunch, as the Auster took off from the field it stalled and struck a tree.[5] It came down very heavily and its undercarriage collapsed. A fire broke out, and the Land Girls ran to see if they could help. Some soldiers quickly appeared on the scene and tried to smash their way into the cockpit to save the pilot but their efforts were in vain. The Land Girls were greatly distressed by what they had witnessed:

When it was clear that there was no hope, we all trooped silently back, tears streaming down our faces.

They were in no condition to return to work that day, and so they were sent back to their hostel in Beaulieu. Nancy Jones said a prayer for the young pilot.

25. A Taylorcraft Auster observation plane, similar to the one which crashed at Exbury on the same day as the Ju 188.

The seven men who had perished in the German bomber crash were buried with full military honours at All Saints Church in Fawley, near Exbury, on 21 April. Their coffins were transported from Calshot on a lorry trailer. Ron Woolhead was one of the men from the RAF base who were detailed onto the burial party and marched the two miles to Fawley. As the funeral procession neared All Saints Church, it passed by the cottage of Margaret Day, whose husband was away serving in the Army. It was a very moving scene.

The Air Force band was playing, and I'm sure that all of us, mostly women and children (many in tears), were full of sorrow and sympathy for the German mothers and families.

A number of local people attended the funeral service and the burials, which were marked by the firing of rifles at the graveside by the guard of honour from RAF Calshot.

And so were laid to rest the seven men who had been travelling on board the lone German bomber as it made its fateful flight to the Hampshire coast early on the morning of 18 April 1944. But a mystery had been born which was to intrigue people for many years to come.

26. The funeral service was held at All Saints Church in Fawley on 21 April 1944.

27. The seven men were buried with full military honours.

CHAPTER 3

Investigation and Speculation

As a result of the investigation which followed the shooting down of the German bomber at Exbury, the 'kill' was credited jointly to the RAF and to Anti-Aircraft Command. The daily report of *Anti-Aircraft Operations against Enemy Aircraft* for 18 April 1944 stated that the Junkers had been engaged by heavy and light anti-aircraft fire, and by anti-aircraft light machine guns on the Isle of Wight and on the Hampshire mainland, at heights of between 100 and 700ft. Tracer hits were seen and pieces of the aircraft were reported to have fallen into the sea. The gun crew manning the Bofors at Lower Exbury certainly claimed to have hit the tail of the Junkers as it was on its way down. The two Typhoons of 266 Squadron were officially considered to have completed the destruction of the enemy aircraft using their 20mm cannons, which were loaded with ball ammunition.[1] The RAF inspection of the wrecked German bomber found 20mm strikes in the tail unit and rear part of the fuselage.[2] In addition to the aircraft of 266 Squadron, two Spitfires of 313 Squadron and four Typhoons of 439 and 197 Squadrons were reported to have been detailed to intercept the Junkers.[3]

Two Air Ministry reports were produced following the German bomber crash. Firstly, a technical assessment of the aircraft, which had been carried out at the crash site. Secondly, an examination of the circumstances surrounding the incident, incorporating information obtained from the interrogation of a Ju 188 pilot from the same Luftwaffe unit as the one to which the Exbury Junkers had belonged.[4]

The identification marking on the sides of the downed Ju 188 was found to be Z6 EK. The 'Z6' indicated that the aircraft belonged to *Kampfgeschwader* 66 (KG66) and the 'K' denoted subordination to the unit's second *Staffel*, ie. 2./KG66.[5] The 'E' was the unique designator of that particular aircraft. A document found in the wreckage showed that the Ju 188s in the *Staffel* 2./KG66 had been designated from Z6 AK to Z6 MK. The camouflage on the upper surface of the German plane was the customary mottled dark-green and light-blue, roughly in equal proportions. Its under-surface had been spray-painted black over the usual light-blue. The reason for this will become apparent later on.

PERSONAL COMBAT REPORT.

STATISTICAL.

Date.	.....18th..April.1944...
Squadron.	.....266.(.Rhodesia.)...
Type and mark of a/c.	.....Typhoon.1B.........
Time up and down.	.....0705...0755........
Time of attack.	........0745............
Place of attack.	....Exbury,.Hants.......
Height of enemy on first sighting	......1000.feet.........
Own height at first sighting.	......1500.feet.........
Enemy casualties	.1.Ju..188.(dest).shared by.F/L.A.V.Sanders.and.. .....F/Sgt.D.H.Dodd....
Our casualties.	........Nil.............

F/L A.V. SANDERS. 266 Rhodesia Squadron.

At 07_45 on the 18th April, I was returning from a sortie in Exercise "Smash" leading a section of four a/c. We had already passed over the S.E.-N.W. runway at base and were flying in line astern preparing to land. I did not then know that there was an enemy a/c in the vicinity. The first intimation I had was a line of heavy A/A bursts in front of me at about 1500 ft. above, behind and slightly to starboard of an a/c which I thought to be a Ju. 188. It was then about a mile away flying from east to west at about 1000ft. The a/c turned to port and I turned inside it to investigate it and confirmed that it was a Ju. 188. By this time I was flying at about 500 ft. and clearly recognised the markings. I experienced some slight return fire from the a/c. Closing in, I opened fire at about 200 yds. with slight deflection from port side and saw strikes on the cockpit and the port wing root, followed by flame and smoke from this area. As I flew over the a/c, I noticed pieces falling from it, and next saw it burning on the ground with a heavy column of smoke rising from it.

My a/c was loaded with ball ammunition and I fired 100 rounds.

Signed ...A.V. Sanders...F/Lt......

28. F/Lt Vernon Sanders's combat report.[6]

Speculation was rife in the aftermath of the Junkers crash at Exbury. The first thing that had struck many of those who had witnessed the carnage at the crash site was the number of bodies which had been found in and around the wrecked bomber. Why had there been as many as seven men on board this plane? The normal crew complement of a Ju 188 was thought to be just four. How on earth had they all managed to fit into the cockpit? The other question being asked was: what had caused the German bomber to fly alone to this part of southern England in broad daylight and to loiter over an area of such importance to the Allies' D-Day preparations?

Several theories initially were advanced. A number of the servicemen at HMS Mastodon believed that the Junkers had been conducting photo-reconnaissance of the invasion fleet, which was building up in the Solent and the Beaulieu river. The extra men, it was suggested, might have been needed to operate the cameras. A more intriguing view, held by a number of people, was that the men on board the German bomber were Slavs, who had been attempting to escape the Nazi regime. It was common knowledge that identity discs and papers found at the crash site had revealed several Slavonic names among the seven men who had been on board the Junkers. Years later, this idea was to be embellished by the author Nevil Shute in his novel *Requiem for a Wren.*

Over time, other ingredients were added to this mystery, as details of the Ju 188's strange behaviour emerged. Jock Leal, who had witnessed these events from the Royal Observer Corps post on the Isle of Wight, later summed things up:

> *Why had it dropped red flares? Why had the pilot not tried to evade gunfire and fighters? Why fly so slowly and so low? Why not defend itself? We asked ourselves the questions but could give no answers.*[7]

In the following chapters, there will be a thorough examination of all the circumstances surrounding this wartime incident, and an attempt will be made to discover the intentions of the seven men who were travelling on board the Ju 188, as it made its ill-fated flight to the Hampshire coast.

29. L/Observer Jock Leal of the Royal Observer Corps. He and his colleagues had been mystified by the behaviour of the lone German bomber early on the morning of 18 April 1944.

CHAPTER 4

The Mystery of the Seven Men

Much of the mystery surrounding the Junkers crash at Exbury concerned the fact that there had been an unusually large number of men on board the German plane. Just who were the seven men who had climbed into the cockpit of the Ju 188 at Avord, in central France, at daybreak on 18 April 1944? Were some of them indeed of Slavonic origin, as their identity discs and papers had seemed to suggest?

As is commonly the case, the truth about the men's identities was rather less dramatic than the speculation which had abounded in the aftermath of the bomber crash. All seven were, in fact, *bona fide* members of the Luftwaffe. Admittedly, two of their surnames were Slavonic, but this merely reflected the fact that these men had been recruited to the Luftwaffe from the far-flung corners of the German Reich. Three of the men were from Germany itself. Two were from Austria, one from East Prussia and one from Sudetenland.[1]

Four of the seven men who died at Exbury were regular members of the same aircrew. A fifth man apparently had the misfortune to be standing in for the final regular crew member. Strangely, the additional two men on board the Junkers were ground crew. All seven served with the bomber unit *2./Kampfgeschwader 66*, as the side-marking of the aircraft had indicated. The following information about the seven men has been gleaned from official Luftwaffe records and, in the case of four of them, from their surviving relatives.

Johann (Hans) Czipin

Unteroffizier Hans Czipin was the Ju 188's 21-year-old pilot (*Flugzeugführer*). He was born on 13 July 1922 in Grafenbach, in Lower Austria, and had been a student at the time of joining the Luftwaffe. Having completed his basic flying training in June 1942, he obtained his advanced pilot's licence in January 1943, and completed further training in late February that year. His first operational posting was to the bomber unit *Kampfgeschwader 6* (KG6) in March 1943, and he was probably stationed initially at Brétigny in France. He was transferred to the second *Staffel* of KG66 (2./KG66) on 5 March 1944.[2]

Johann Krause

Unteroffizier Johann Krause was the bomber's observer (*Beobachter*).[3] He was born on 24 June 1920 in Sternberg in Sudetenland (known as Sternberk in today's Czech Republic) and, at 23, was the oldest and most experienced member of the crew. His first operational posting was to the sixth *Staffel* of KG26, a torpedo-bomber unit, in May 1941, and he was wounded when his aircraft crashed in Crete in January 1942. Krause attended the pilot training school in Dortmund between July 1942 and January 1943 and, during the following two months, he was assigned to a test unit in Jüterbog. In April 1943 he was posted to the bomber unit KG6, and in mid-November that year he embarked on further training at pilot school A41. Along with his fellow crew members from KG6, he was transferred to 2./KG66 on 5 March 1944.[4]

Robert Schultes

Unteroffizier Robert Schultes was born in Vienna on 26 May 1924, and was the crew's radio operator (*Bordfunker*). Details of his military career are very sparse, but he joined his first operational bomber unit, KG6, as a qualified radio operator in mid-April 1943. He, too, was posted to 2./KG66 in early March 1944. At just 19, Robert Schultes was the youngest member of the crew.[5]

30. Eitel Wysotzki

Eitel Wysotzki

Twenty-two-year-old *Unteroffizier* Eitel Wysotzki was one of the crew's two air gunners (*Bordschütze*). He was born on 7 May 1921, and came from Seegutten in the Johannisburg district of East Prussia (known as Nowe Guty in today's Poland). He qualified as an air gunner in January 1943, and was posted to his first operational unit, KG6, in April 1943, at roughly the same time as Robert Schultes and Johann Krause. He was transferred to 2./KG66 with Krause, Schultes and Hans Czipin in March 1944.[6]

31. Hans Ehrhardt

Hans Ehrhardt

The second air gunner, *Obergefreiter* Hans Ehrhardt, was born in Ilmenau in eastern Germany on 20 March 1922. An only child, Hans had joined the Hitler Youth organisation at the age of 11. When he left school, he trained as a hairdresser. However, his interest in flying was so great that he had wanted to interrupt his training to join Hitler's '*Legion Condor*' in support of General Franco, during the Spanish Civil War, but his mother would not allow him to go.[7]

After completing his training, Hans went into military service. He joined the Luftwaffe in 1941, and trained as an air gunner with a regiment at Crailsheim. Following further gunnery training, he was assigned to the bomber unit KG6 in June 1943. Having initially been stationed at Brétigny in France, he was posted to Chièvres in Belgium in late January 1944, and transferred to 2./KG66 in the middle of the following month. Hans had been married at Easter in 1943 and, at the time of his death, his wife Elfriede was expecting their first child.[8]

32. Hans married Elfriede at Easter in 1943.

33. Hans Ehrhardt's grave at Fawley.

Hans Ehrhardt was not a regular member of this particular Ju 188 crew, but happened to be standing in for a sick crewman on the ill-fated flight of 18 April 1944. He was 22 at the time of his death.[9]

34. Leonhard Schwingenstein as a student in 1941.

Leonhard Schwingenstein

Obergefreiter Leonhard Schwingenstein was a member of the ground crew of 2./KG66. He was born in Augsburg on 17 March 1921 and had one sister, Maria. After finishing his school education, he spent three-and-a-half years studying mechanical engineering. Then, at the outbreak of war, he was conscripted into National Work Service. He attended the Rudolf Diesel Engineering School in Augsburg, and subsequently underwent practical training at the Dornier works in Friedrichshafen-Bodensee.[10]

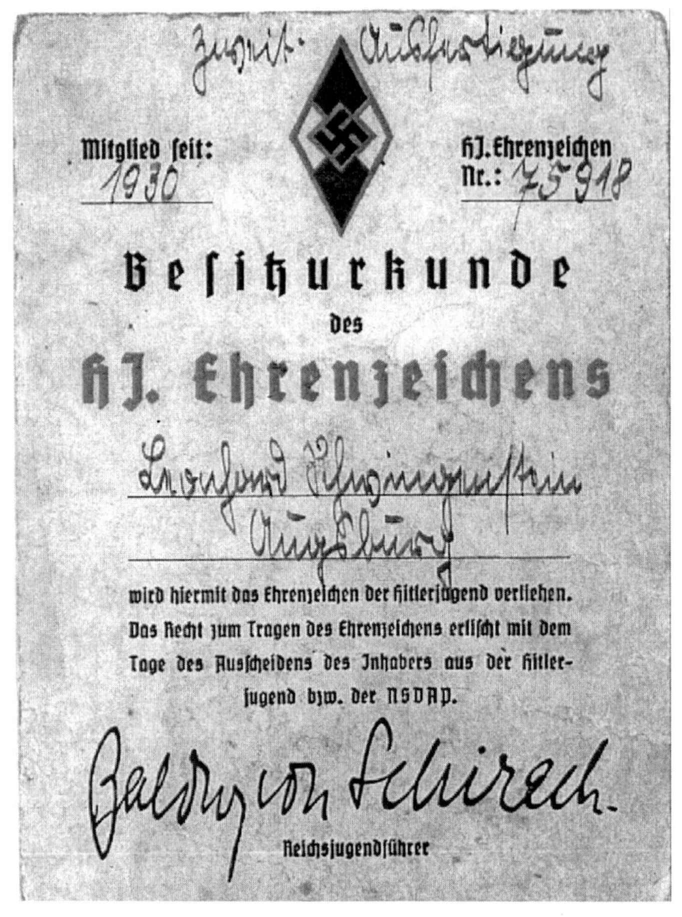

Mitglied seit: 1930

HJ.-Ehrenzeichen Nr.: 75918

Besitzurkunde

des

HJ. Ehrenzeichens

wird hiermit das Ehrenzeichen der Hitlerjugend verliehen. Das Recht zum Tragen des Ehrenzeichens erlischt mit dem Tage des Ausscheidens des Inhabers aus der Hitler-jugend bzw. der NSDAP.

Baldur von Schirach

Reichsjugendführer

35. Leonhard's Hitler Youth certificate.

Leonhard was very interested in aviation, and he went on to study at the Aeronautical Engineering School in Thorn (Torun in today's Poland). In the final term of 1943, along with the rest of the school, he signed up for military service, and joined the Luftwaffe as an aircraft mechanic. He was assigned to 2./KG66 as a *1. Wart (*Chief Ground Crew).[11]

Although he was officially a member of the ground crew, according to his family Leonhard had already flown in a bomber on a previous mission. On completion of three such flights he was to have been awarded an Iron Cross First Class. Leonhard was 23 at the time of his death.[12]

36. Leonhard Schwingenstein's grave at Fawley.

Edgar Vester

Twenty-year-old *Gefreiter* Edgar Vester was the second member of the ground crew travelling on board the Ju 188. Born on 3 September 1923, Edgar came from Dortmund, and was the son of an engineer. He had one sister Brigitte. He joined the Hitler Youth organisation at the age of 11 and, after his school education, he attended a technical college where he learned the trade of bricklayer. He was recruited to the German armed forces in June 1941. At his initial fitness examination, he expressed a wish to undertake air intelligence duties, and he was considered suitable for this line of work. He was also later considered for training as a radio operator.[13]

Having completed a period of work service as a labourer, Edgar joined the Luftwaffe in April 1942. He was initially stationed at Werl, just east of Dortmund, where he trained as a radio technician (*Funkwart*). His work involved the removal, repair, re-installation and testing of airborne radio equipment. In October that year he was posted to the Air Intelligence Office at Goslar and, in mid-February 1943, he was transferred to the Air

Intelligence Office in Flensburg, close to the German border with Denmark. From March to September 1943 he was assigned to a Luftwaffe unit in southern France, then underwent two further periods of practical training, first at Leipzig, then at an Air Intelligence school at Wollin in Pomerania.[14]

37. Edgar Vester

In addition to being a radio technician, Edgar had also trained as an aircrew radio operator. However, he had not been able to pass the tests because of a problem with his eyesight. In a letter to his parents in January 1944, he indicated that he was not actually aircrew and had never taken part in a bombing raid over England, which he called the *witches' cauldron*. He had, however, flown on several test flights to check the radios on various aircraft, including Messerschmitts and Junkers, following their repair.[15]

Edgar Vester was assigned to the ground crew of the bomber unit 2./KG66 in November 1943. He was initially stationed at Montdidier in northern France, then re-located to Avord in central France probably in late March 1944.[16]

What, then, can be deduced about the men who were on board the German bomber which crashed at Exbury? Firstly, at ages between 19 and 23, they seemed a very young crew. However, the list of losses suffered by 2./KG66 between January and mid-April 1944 suggests that the average age of this crew was, in fact, only slightly younger than the average age of the other crews in the *Staffel*.[17] Secondly, these men were of relatively junior rank – none of them being more senior than *Unteroffizier*, which was roughly equivalent to the rank of RAF Corporal.[18] Again, though, this was not as remarkable as it might first have seemed. A review of the *Staffel*'s losses between January and mid-April 1944 shows several other instances of Ju 188 crews being of *Unteroffizier* rank and below; these included a Ju 188 (side marking Z6 CK) which was shot down at Montdidier on 2 January, and its replacement which was lost on the same day as the Exbury Junkers.[19]

The five aircrew had all been assigned to the bomber unit KG6 in 1943, prior to their posting to KG66, and it is almost certain that four of them - Czipin (pilot), Krause (observer), Schultes (radio operator) and Wysotzki (one of the air gunners) - had been together as a crew for a year or so before the events of 18 April 1944. They were certainly transferred to KG66 on the same date. Whilst Hans Ehrhardt, the second gunner, was in the same *Staffel*, he belonged to a different Ju 188 crew, and had been transferred from KG6 to KG66 earlier in 1944.

38. Hans Ehrhardt, one of the gunners, had followed the same path from KG6 to KG66 as the other four aircrew members, but he actually belonged to a different crew. He had the greatest misfortune to be standing in for a sick crewman on the final flight of Ju 188 Z6 EK.

It is not clear just how much experience of the war this young crew would have had. The service records of all five aircrew members, together with documents found in the wreckage at Exbury, indicate that they had been posted initially to the fourth *Gruppe* of KG6 (ie. IV/KG6) at Brétigny, south of Paris. This was a supplementary or supply unit, which provided operational training for crews before they were moved into the three front-line *Gruppen* (ie. I-III/KG6).[20]

The identity discs found on the young men who perished at Exbury indicated that the four regular crew members had, at some stage, been transferred from the training *Gruppe* of KG6 to front-line duties in the first *Gruppe;* in the third *Staffel* (3./KG6), to be precise.[21] Depending on the timing of this move, they may have been deployed to Italy at some point in 1943, and would definitely have seen some action there. Certainly, Johann Krause, the observer, was particularly experienced. He had flown in several front-line bomber units over the previous three years, he had been wounded when his plane crashed in Crete in 1942, and was probably the owner of the Iron Cross which was taken from the crash site by a sailor from HMS Mastodon.[22]

But why were as many as seven men all travelling on the same plane? Despite the official crew complement for the Junkers Ju 188 being four, casualty figures for all aircraft of this type, which were shot down over Britain between January and mid-April 1944, actually indicate that a crew of five was the norm during that period.[23] The list of losses suffered specifically by 2./KG66 in that time also confirms a five-man crew for the Ju 188.[24] So, there is nothing remarkable in the fact that there were five aircrew on this particular aircraft.

The sixth and seventh men - Schwingenstein and Vester - were, in fact, members of the ground crew of 2./KG66. Whilst their presence on the Ju 188, which flew to England on 18 April 1944, seems highly peculiar and has caused much speculation over the years, it can fairly easily be explained. The answer lies in the fact that the Junkers was meant to have flown from its base at Avord in central France up to Soesterberg in Holland, from where a bombing raid on London was to have been mounted that night. Several maps were found in the wreckage at Exbury with the route from Avord to Soesterberg clearly marked.[25] At that stage in the war, the Luftwaffe's policy of using advanced airfields from which to mount attacks on Britain apparently required the transportation of some ground crew from the bomber unit's rear base, so that the aircraft could be serviced by their own technicians at these forward airfields. This is borne out in Leonhard Schwingenstein's last letter to his mother, just five days before his death, when he wrote that he was away from his normal location for a few days at a time.

39. It was not unprecedented for the Ju 188s of 2./KG66 to carry ground crew on the flight from the rear base to the advanced airfield.

A pilot from the same *Staffel*, who had been shot down and taken prisoner in February 1944, told British intelligence officers investigating the Exbury Junkers incident that, whilst it was normally forbidden for more than five crew to be carried on board a Ju 188, he had transported seven men in his aircraft (including two ground crew) during a deployment to Soesterberg in Holland.[26] His radio operator, *Unteroffizier* Helmut Thomale, has also recently confirmed that it was not unprecedented to ferry ground crew on the flight to the advanced airfield. The bombers of 2./KG66 relied heavily on radio navigation aids, and it was vital to have technicians at the forward base to service this equipment. The specialist role of 2./KG66 will be explained in more detail in the next chapter.

Astonishment at the number of bodies found in the wreckage of the crashed Junkers at Exbury was accompanied by surprise that seven men had all been able to fit into the cockpit. The writer Nevil Shute later captured this sentiment when he fictionalised the mysterious Ju 188 flight in his novel *Requiem for a Wren:*

> *Craigie asked, 'How many of them were in it?'*
> *'Seven.'*
> *'Seven? I thought the Ju 188 had a crew of four.'*
> *'So did I. Go and count them, if you like. They must have been jammed in, sitting on each other's knees.'* [27]

One of the more colourful theories to have been advanced on this subject is that three of the men could have been carried in a special canister, which the Germans had developed to transport secret agents. The canister was dropped by parachute and Ju 188s had been used for this purpose.[28]

40. *Unteroffizier* Helmut Thomale, a Ju 188 radio operator from the same *Staffel* as the Exbury Junkers. Ground crew had also been carried on his aircraft during deployments to the forward airfield at Soesterberg.

But the truth is that, whilst it may not have been overly comfortable, it was perfectly possible to accommodate seven men in the cockpit of a Ju 188, which was more spacious than that of its predecessor, the Ju 88. This was recently confirmed by Helmut Thomale, a radio operator who also served with 2./KG66.

The pilot's and observer's seats were alongside each other in the forward part of the cockpit (pilot on the left, observer on the right). The radio operator's position was at the back of the cockpit, facing to the rear. There were two locations for the gunners, in the ventral and dorsal positions. According to Helmut Thomale, one of the ground crew could have been positioned between the pilot and the observer in the front of the cockpit, and the other on an emergency seat behind the pilot. Helmut Thomale explains that the latter was the location from where the 'Gee' receiver was operated on his aircraft. Although not all of the Ju 188s in the *Staffel* 2./KG66 were equipped with this navigational aid, there was space for an additional body in that position.

So, it seems that there was nothing particularly mysterious about the number of men travelling on board the German bomber early on that April morning, nor about how they had all managed to fit into the cockpit. However, the question as to why they made that flight to the Hampshire coast, alone in broad daylight, and right into the heart of the preparations for the Normandy landings, is an entirely different proposition altogether.

41. Is this the aircrew of Ju 188 Z6 EK, which flew its last mission on 18 April 1944? This photograph, which is in the possession of the family of Eitel Wysotzki, was taken at a studio in Brussels. The date is unknown. Eitel Wysotzki, one of the gunners on the Junkers, is probably seated on the left. The *Gefreiter* pictured on the right of the group also appears to be wearing an air gunner's badge. He may be the second gunner, whom Hans Ehrhardt replaced on the fateful flight. The other three men pictured (all holding the *Unteroffizier* rank) could be Hans Czipin (pilot), Johann Krause (observer) and Robert Schultes (radio operator).

CHAPTER 5

The Luftwaffe Perspective

Before investigating this wartime puzzle in greater detail, it is important to consider the historical context in which it occurred. In particular, it is necessary to learn a little more about the Junkers Ju 188, the role of the Luftwaffe unit to which this particular aircraft and its crew belonged, and to understand the type of operations in which the unit was involved at that stage in the war.

Firstly, some background about the plane itself. The Ju 188 was an evolution of the highly-successful Ju 88, which the Luftwaffe had been using since the beginning of the Second World War. It was originally designed as a dive-bomber but later put to other uses, such as level-flight bombing, pathfinding, reconnaissance and anti-ship operations. In all, approximately 1,100 Ju 188s were built.

The Ju 188 was faster than its predecessor, the Ju 88, being capable of speeds in excess of 300mph. It also had a better rate of climb, and could operate at altitudes above 30,000ft. Whilst the Ju 188 A and D types were powered by Junkers Jumo engines, the E variant, of the type which crashed at Exbury, was fitted with BMW-801 radials.

As already mentioned, the Ju 188 cockpit was more spacious than that of the Ju 88, and it had a more extensive perspex surround. Its wings were a further distinguishing feature since they were more pointed than those of the Ju 88.[1] Several of the eyewitnesses to the events of 18 April 1944 had recognised the German aircraft as a Ju 188 on account of this feature.

42. The cockpit of the Ju 188 was unmistakable with its extensive perspex surround.

43. A page from the Royal Observer Corps German aircraft recognition book, featuring the Ju 88 (left) and the Ju 188 (right). The main distinguishing features of the latter were its pointed wing-tips and its bulbous perspex cockpit surround.

The first few Ju 188s were deployed to *Erprobungs Kommando 188* in May 1943. This was the unit whose task it was to introduce the new bomber into service. Operational testing continued into the summer, and the Ju 188 was first used in anger in mid-August 1943 for a night raid on a factory in Lincoln. By early October, the first *Gruppe* of KG6 had completed the transition to the new aircraft, and it became operational at Chièvres in Belgium. The Ju 188 was first flown in a raid on London on 15 October 1943.[2]

KG66 had just one *Gruppe*, ie. I/KG66, comprising three *Staffeln*. This unit had been formed in Chartres in May 1943 as an independent bomber wing. It was directly subordinate to *IX Fliegerkorps*, whose commander, *Oberst* Dietrich Peltz, had been charged with directing the air war against Britain. The new unit, I/KG66, was assigned a specialist pathfinding and target-marking role in support of the bomber force of *IX Fliegerkorps*. At this stage in the war, Luftwaffe raids on Britain were possible only on moonless nights because of the very strong fighter and anti-aircraft defences; hence the need for specialist pathfinder support. I/KG66 was equipped initially with Ju 88 and Dornier Do 217 bombers.[3]

44. Dietrich Peltz, *Angriffsführer England.*

In order to counter the increasing threat from British air defences, especially night fighters, new tactics were developed for the pathfinder aircraft of I/KG66, incorporating specific approach and exit routes, altitudes and speeds, and these measures also involved the use of *Düppel* tin foil to jam British radar, like the RAF's use of 'Window'. Target-marking for the bomber force was carried out using parachute-retarded flares.[4]

Initially, I/KG66 depended on a combination of the X and Y radio navigation aids to support its route- and target-marking roles. These methods, which relied on the use of approach beams, had been employed by the Luftwaffe since the early days of the war, and both systems were susceptible to jamming.[5] By the end of 1943, I/KG66 had moved to Montdidier in northern France and its second *Staffel*, 2./KG66, converted from Ju 88 to Ju 188 aircraft.

45. A Ju 188 E of I/KG66 at Montdidier in northern France.

Two new radio navigation aids were introduced at around this time; these went by the covernames of *Egon* and *Truhe*. The former was highly accurate and similar in method to the British 'Oboe' system.[6] Its advantage was that the pathfinder aircraft were not tied to an approach beam and therefore there was more opportunity to practise deception *en route* to the target.[7]

Truhe was a pirated version of the RAF's 'Gee' navigation system.[8] It was initially developed for use by the Luftwaffe from equipment and maps acquired from RAF bombers which had been shot down over Germany. The attraction of *Truhe* to the Luftwaffe was that it was a passive system, with receivers on board the German bombers picking up the signals transmitted from Britain, and therefore there was no risk of jamming. However, a drawback was that the equipment took up a lot of room and required an additional crew member.

After several German aircraft carrying 'Gee' receivers had been shot down, the British realised that the RAF system had been copied, and made some modifications. This made it more difficult for the Luftwaffe to use.[9]

46. *Unteroffizier* Helmut Thomale, a radio operator with the pathfinder unit 2./KG66. His Ju 188 was shot down on the night of 24 February 1944. He and his pilot were the only crew members to survive, and spent the rest of the war in captivity.

Helmut Thomale, a radio operator with 2./KG66, whose Ju 188 had been shot down over southern England on the night of 24 February 1944, remembers flying with his crew to Köthen in eastern Germany in late 1943, in order for their Ju 188 to be fitted with a 'Gee' receiver. When their Junkers was shot down, this equipment was discovered by British air intelligence officers.

In a letter to his mother shortly before his death, Leonhard Schwingenstein, one of the ground crew travelling on the Ju 188 which crashed at Exbury, had written that German civilians were no safer from Allied air raids in bad weather than when conditions were clear. When visibility was poor, German defences were hampered but the British were *laughing*. This warning was probably based on his knowledge of the RAF's 'Gee' navigation system, which the pathfinders of I/KG66 were, by now, also exploiting. An RAF 'Gee' map of the Paris-Geneva region was found in the burnt-out wreckage of the Ju 188 at Exbury.[10]

Between March and May 1944 elements of I/KG66, including the second *Staffel*, were stationed at Avord, near Bourges in central France. As already mentioned, it is certain that the Junkers which flew alone to the Hampshire coast on 18 April 1944 had set off from Avord that morning.[11]

47. *Reichsmarschall* Hermann Göring, Commander-in-Chief of the Luftwaffe, was responsible for planning the retaliatory raids against Britain. The operation was codenamed *Steinbock*.

By the time of the Ju 188 crash at Exbury in mid-April 1944, the pathfinders of I/KG66 had, for several months, been involved in a series of raids on Britain, which had been codenamed *Steinbock* (literally 'Ibex'). This operation also came to be known as the *little blitz.*

In late 1943 Hitler had ordered an operation to be mounted to intensify the air war against Britain, in retaliation for the devastating Allied air attacks on German cities, especially Berlin. *Reichsmarschall* Hermann

Göring, Commander-in-Chief of the Luftwaffe, was charged with drawing up plans for this retaliatory action.[12]

On 3 December 1943, following a high-level conference, Göring issued a set of orders to his Chiefs of Staff, calling for *concentrated attacks on cities and especially industrial centres and ports*, in order to avenge the *terror attacks by the enemy*. The operation, codenamed *Steinbock*, was to commence *at the end of the full moon period in December*. As a security measure, the raids were to be mounted only from advanced airfields, with the bomber units' main and reserve staffs to be moved back to rear bases. Seventy percent of the bomb payload was to consist of incendiaries (in retaliation for the Allied air tactics), and the heaviest bombs (over 1,000kg) were to be loaded with a special high-explosive *England mixture*. Over 500 aircraft were assembled for this new bomber offensive; these preparations included the despatch of four bomber *Gruppen* from the Italian theatre to the Luftwaffe's Western Command.[13]

Helmut Thomale remembers the crews from the pathfinder unit 2./KG66 being briefed about the impending intensification of the air war against Britain. One morning in early December 1943, probably the 9th or 10th of the month, they were taken by bus from their base at Montdidier, in northern France, to the air base at Laon, some 80 miles to the east. They had not been told in advance where they were going. In a large hangar at the air base, the crews of I/KG66 were joined by those from other bomber units of *IX Fliegerkorps*, including KG2 and KG6. At around midday a Junkers Ju 52 transport aircraft arrived, escorted by two Messerschmitt Me 109s. Much to the men's surprise, out stepped *Reichsmarschall* Göring accompanied by *Generalfeldmarschall* Hugo Sperrle, commander of the Luftwaffe's western grouping, *Luftflotte 3*. The VIPs inspected the aircrews, and each airman had to report how many missions he had flown against the enemy. A number of medals were awarded. Later, Göring gave an address to the assembled crews, in which he announced the new campaign, although he did not tell the men exactly when it was to begin. He swore that this would be the biggest possible operation.

In fact, *Steinbock* did not get underway until late January 1944, and it was to prove very costly to the Luftwaffe, with the loss of some 300 bombers and their crews out of an initial force of approximately 500 aircraft. Although a number of heavy raids were mounted on London and major British ports during this campaign, the results were variable, at best, and had little overall impact. *Steinbock* had petered out by the end of May.[14]

The bombing raid of 18/19 April, in which Ju 188 Z6 EK was meant to have taken part, proved to be the last manned Luftwaffe assault on London of the entire war. A bomber force of some 125 aircraft was assembled for this mission, including Ju 88s, Ju 188s, Heinkel He 177s, Dornier Do 217s and Messerschmitt Me 410s. Thirteen German bombers were officially lost, not including the Junkers which had never made it to the forward airfield in Holland.[15]

Helmut Thomale flew on several pathfinding and target-marking missions in support of the bombing raids on Britain during operation *Steinbock*. From late 1943 to early 1944, Helmut's crew was based at Montdidier in northern France. Soesterberg in Holland was used as an advanced airfield on several occasions, when their task was to mark turning points over the North Sea for the main bomber force. The forward deployment to Soesterberg, ahead of the night raid, was conducted at low altitude, and navigation was carried out using compass, maps and visual contact with the ground. The observer provided the pilot with the correct course to fly at the time of take-off. If poor weather was encountered *en route*, then on-board direction-finding and homing equipment could be used by the radio operator in order to ensure that the aircraft did not stray off course.

Correspondence from both members of the ground crew, shortly before their death, reflects the fact that the Luftwaffe was bracing itself for the Allied invasion of France at that time. In a letter written in early April, Edgar Vester, the radio technician, recounted to his parents how *Generalfeldmarschall* Hugo Sperrle had visited I/KG66 at Avord on the first day of the month. Sperrle had expressed his appreciation for the operations carried out by the pathfinder unit and, *in a few brief words*, gave *the final directives for the great struggle* expected in the forthcoming weeks. In his letter, Edgar Vester referred to this period as the *calm before the storm.*

48. *Generalfeldmarschall* Hugo Sperrle, commander of the Luftwaffe's western grouping, *Luftflotte 3*. He had accompanied *Reichsmarschall* Hermann Göring, head of the Luftwaffe, to Laon, where the crews of *IX Fliegerkorps* were briefed on the impending *Steinbock* operation. He also visited the crews of the pathfinder unit I/KG66 at Avord in early April to urge them on in the face of the impending great struggle.

In a letter to his mother just five days before his death, Leonhard Schwingenstein, the other ground technician, had also anticipated the Allied invasion. He had expressed outrage at the Allied air attacks on German civilians and saw a landing by the British as an opportunity for *the homeland* to take its revenge. He predicted that an assault would be made *on the west coast* and that, whilst the British troops might gain a foothold, they could be driven back. He was, nevertheless, wary of the scale of the American air power and felt that the impending Allied action spelt great danger for Germany. If the British put everything into it, this encounter would most likely decide the outcome of the war.

CHAPTER 6

Into the Hornets' Nest

Whilst the Luftwaffe was mounting the *Steinbock* raids, in retaliation for the Allied fire-bombing of German cities, the Allies were making their final plans for the invasion of France, as Edgar Vester and Leonhard Schwingenstein had anticipated in their last letters to their families. The Solent and the Beaulieu river were at the very heart of the British Combined Operations preparations. Not surprisingly, this whole coastal area was completely cordoned off in the run-up to D-Day, as the marshalling of the invasion forces took place amid the tightest security. Thus, it is not an exaggeration to say that, when the lone German bomber loitered over this part of southern England just seven weeks before D-Day, it was flying over some of the locations that would be most critical to the success of the Normandy landings.

At Cowes, on the northern tip of the Isle of Wight, over which the Junkers had circled, was the Operations Headquarters of the commanders of the three British and Canadian forces tasked with assaulting the Normandy beaches in the Gold, Juno and Sword sectors. This HQ was based at HMS Vectis on the premises of the Royal Yacht Squadron.[1]

As the Ju 188 steadily made its way across the Solent, flying well below the broken cloud, its crew could not have failed to notice the huge fleet of Allied landing craft and support vessels assembling in this stretch of water to the north of the Isle of Wight.

Exbury House, close to the Beaulieu river on the Hampshire mainland, over which the Junkers flew twice before crashing in a nearby field, was also of key military importance. The house, which was owned by the Rothschild family, had been requisitioned by the Royal Navy in May

1942, and it was commissioned as the Combined Operations base HMS Mastodon in early 1943. Mastodon was to become closely involved in the planning for the landings in the Gold and Juno sectors on D-Day.[2]

49. Exbury House, owned by the Rothschild family and commissioned by the Royal Navy as HMS Mastodon.

50. The lodge at the entrance to the main drive to Exbury House was used by the Navy as a guardhouse.

In early 1944 preparations for the Normandy landings had quickly gathered pace, and the number of naval personnel stationed at HMS Mastodon increased accordingly. These included more than 100 of the Women's Royal Naval Service (Wrens). By the time of the German bomber's mysterious flight over Exbury in mid-April, the base was positively heaving; the Beaulieu river was becoming packed with landing craft and Mastodon was responsible for servicing most of their requirements. Several thousand naval personnel and Marines, who were temporarily stationed at the base in advance of D-Day, were camped out in tents or quartered in Nissen huts close to the house on the Exbury estate.[3] In his book *The Beaulieu River Goes To War*, Cyril Cunningham gives a comprehensive account of the involvement of Exbury House, and other locations in the Beaulieu river area, in the preparations for the Allied invasion of France.

51. Lepe Beach at Stansore Point – the slipways used to launch the giant Phoenixes into the Solent are still visible.

As the lone German bomber circled low over this part of the Hampshire coast it would also have flown very close to the stretch of Lepe Beach at Stansore Point, where components of the Mulberry harbours were constructed. Six huge concrete structures, called Phoenixes, which were used as parts of the breakwater for the floating harbour, were built there. In all, one hundred and forty-seven Phoenixes were constructed at various locations, mainly in southern England. As each Phoenix was completed on Lepe Beach it was launched sideways down slipways into the Solent. By the end of March 1944, 78% of the Phoenixes required for the two Mulberry harbours had been built and, after pressure was exerted by the Prime Minister in late April, the remainder were finished by 23 May. The completed structures were sent to Selsey and Dungeness.[4] Whilst it is not clear exactly when work on the Phoenixes at Stansore Point was completed, it is possible that several were still being built when the Junkers loitered over this area on 18 April. In any case, there would certainly have been evidence of the major construction work, some of which remains even today.

52. A Phoenix is towed into position at Arromanches.

The other military location which played a crucial part in the curious events of 18 April 1944 was the airfield at Needs Oar Point, at the mouth of the Beaulieu river. This was where the Typhoons of 266 (Rhodesia) Squadron, which intercepted the German bomber, had temporarily been based. The airfield was officially called an Advanced Landing Ground (ALG), one of several such facilities which had been constructed along the south coast in late 1943 as part of the Allies' strategy of moving tactical aircraft to forward airfields ahead of the Normandy landings. From 10 April 1944, Needs Oar Point housed some 120 Typhoon Mk 1B fighter-bombers from four different squadrons of 146 Wing, which was subordinate to 84 Group of the Second Tactical Air Force. This latter formation had been created specifically to support the Allied ground forces for the invasion of France.[5]

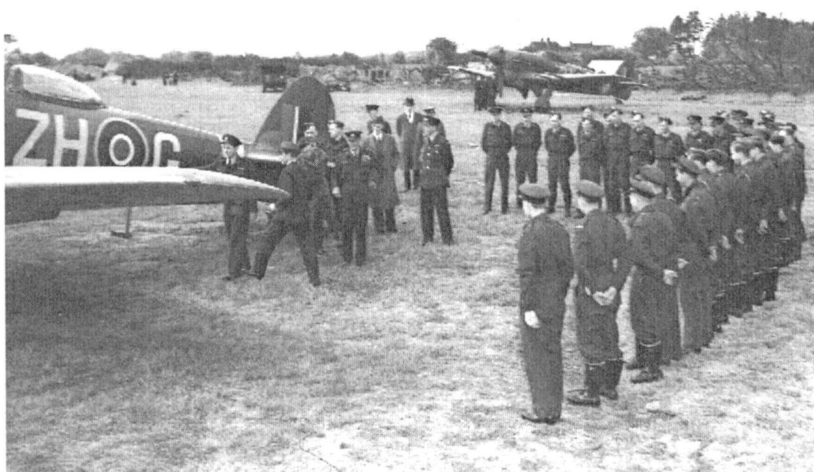

53/54. The Hon. Godfrey Huggins, Prime Minister of Southern Rhodesia, visited 266 (Rhodesia) Squadron at Needs Oar Point on 18 May 1944 to present a Typhoon – a gift from the people of Southern Rhodesia. In the top photograph the PM is pictured trying out a dinghy on dry land, much to the amusement of the pilots of 266 Squadron. F/Sgt Don Dodd, one of the pilots who intercepted the Ju 188, is crouching on the far left.

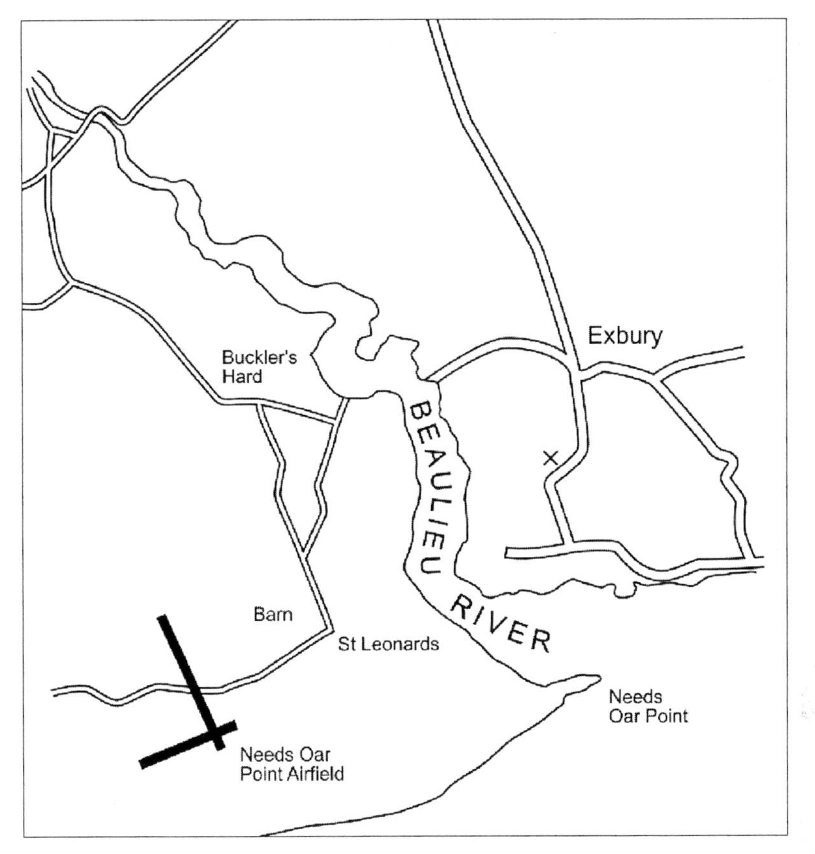

55. Location of the Advanced Landing Ground at Needs Oar Point, close to the Solent and across the Beaulieu river from Exbury.

The ALG at Needs Oar Point was actually situated several hundred yards to the west of the mouth of the Beaulieu river, in the vicinity of Park Farm. Fields were flattened and hedges removed to make way for the airfield. Sommerfeld steel tracking was laid down for the runways, and most of the pilots and ground crew lived in tents. Light anti-aircraft guns were installed to protect the airfield.[6] The heavy guns of 356 HAA battery were later deployed to an adjacent field, in May 1944, as part of the anti-aircraft protection for the invasion marshalling area in the New Forest.

56/57. Looking south towards the Isle of Wight, a plaque now marks the spot where the north-south runway of the Needs Oar Point Advanced Landing Ground crossed the road between East End and St Leonards, close to the Solent. This is one of several plaques commemorating wartime airfields in the New Forest, which have been painstakingly produced by local historian Alan Brown.

Over the years, many people have expressed the view that the German bomber's curious flight to this part of the southern coast of England on 18 April 1944 must have been connected with the importance of these military locations to the Allies' preparations for D-Day. Also, it has been suggested that, if the Ju 188 had been allowed to escape, its crew would have reported what they seen of the invasion preparations, and that this would have seriously undermined *Operation Fortitude*, the Allies' plan to deceive the Germans into thinking that the main thrust of the assault would be mounted from south-east England against the Pas de Calais. In fact, by early May 1944, the German High Command had received reports of a build-up of landing craft north of the Isle of Wight, but this still did not enable it to form a clear picture of the precise intentions of the Allies. More of this later.

CHAPTER 7

The Blurring of Fiction and Fact

That the mystery of the Exbury Junkers incident has endured over the years can partly be credited to the writer Nevil Shute. His novel *Requiem for a Wren*, which was published in 1955, has a fictional account of this wartime episode as its centrepiece. The incident also appeared in Shute's earlier unpublished novel *Blind Understanding*.[1]

58. Lt-Cdr Nevil Shute Norway, RNVR, was greatly fascinated by the strange events of 18 April 1944.

Nevil Shute, whose real name was Nevil Shute Norway, was an engineer by trade, and he had made a name for himself designing and developing rockets, torpedoes and other weaponry. By the time war broke out in 1939, he had also written several popular novels. He joined the Royal Naval Volunteer Reserve (RNVR) in 1940 and, once his engineering background had come to light, he was posted to the Admiralty, where he was commissioned as a Lieutenant and assigned to the Department of Miscellaneous Weapon Development. This Department was responsible for developing precisely the type of weapons with which he had previously been involved as a civilian.[2]

Now promoted to the rank of Lieutenant-Commander, Shute worked in the Beaulieu river area of Hampshire, at various times between the autumn of 1943 and spring 1944, on devices which were intended to assist the Allied landings on the Normandy beaches. In his book *The Beaulieu River Goes To War*, Cyril Cunningham provides a detailed account of Nevil Shute's connections with HMS Mastodon and his involvement with the D-Day preparations in the Beaulieu river area.[3]

However, it was Lt-Cdr Norway's role as a war correspondent for the Ministry of Information, in the run-up to D-Day, which brought about his involvement with the Exbury Junkers incident. In an unpublished Ministry of Information article, *Second Front – III*, he describes how he had taken part in an invasion exercise off the south coast of England, on board a tank landing craft (LCT). The exercise had ended early in the morning:

> *I left that L.C.T at the same hard as the Canadians and got in to my truck and drove away. Only a few miles on I came on an enigma of this curious war, in a small country lane with fields on either side, very near the sea. A German aeroplane, a Ju 188, had crashed across the road that morning; it had spread itself over the field in the manner of a modern aircraft, so that no part of it was recognisable or more than one foot high above the ground, save for the rudder.*[4]

As Shute had not witnessed the crash himself, he seems to have obtained most of his information about it from a young Air Force officer who *was doing a technical examination of the black, burned wreckage*. He was told that the Junkers had come in from the sea at an altitude of 1,000ft and in broad daylight. He was informed that the bomber had been attacked by several anti-aircraft batteries, and that one gunner captain had sworn that he personally had put seven Bofors shells into it. He also heard how four Typhoons returning from a fighter sweep had caught up with the Junkers and *gave it their squirts*. Shute ends the Ministry of Information article by contemplating some of the puzzling elements of this incident:

> *What duty brought these seven NCOs to England in full daylight, without bombs, and at that suicidal height? Why seven? Or had they stolen the machine, and were they trying to escape to England to surrender? It may well be that we shall never hear the answers.*[5]

59. *A small country lane, with fields on either side, very near the sea.* But it was a very different scene which confronted Nevil Shute, when he turned the corner into this stretch of the Lower Exbury road on the morning of 18 April 1944.

This *enigma of a curious war*, which Nevil Shute had encountered whilst driving through Exbury seven weeks before D-Day, obviously had a profound and lasting effect on him. In 1948 he wove the wartime mystery into the novel *Blind Understanding*. In this unpublished work, Janet Payne, an Ordnance Wren, whose job is to service Oerlikon anti-aircraft guns on landing craft, shoots down a German plane. Her excitement turns to sorrow when she learns that the aircraft was carrying a German who was her father's old student and assistant and who, like the other men travelling on the plane, had been working for the Allies as an agent in Germany.[6]

60. A first-edition copy of *Requiem for a Wren*, published in 1955. The artwork was by Val Biro, who illustrated the dust-jackets on the Heinemann editions of a number of Nevil Shute's novels. Val Biro is also well-known as a children's author.

This theme was re-worked when it appeared as the centrepiece of Shute's later novel *Requiem for a Wren*, which was published in 1955, eleven years after the Junkers crash at Exbury. In this book, Janet Prentice, a crack-shot Wren who services Oerlikon guns on tank landing craft in the Beaulieu river, shoots down a Ju 188 bomber. Her elation soon turns to anguish when she learns that the seven men on board were Poles or Czechs, who were thought to have stolen the Junkers in order to escape to England. Janet Prentice views the series of personal tragedies, which subsequently befall her, as divine retribution for the awful deed which she has done. She finally commits suicide, believing that justice will not fully be done until she has taken her own life.

In Nevil Shute's account of the shooting down of the Ju 188 in *Requiem for a Wren*, some of the details of the incident are wholly accurate and others are pure fiction. Whilst the novelist remained faithful to some of the facts, he obviously needed to modify certain aspects in order to engineer the plot.

As far as the date and time of the incident are concerned, there is something of a discrepancy. In *Requiem* the Junkers crash happens on *a Saturday morning at the very end of April*, which would have been 29 April.[7] The real incident occurred on Tuesday 18 April. In the fictional account, the Junkers appears at 11 o'clock in the morning whereas, in real life, the time was approximately 7.30am. However, in both cases it was a bright spring day.

In *Requiem*, Shute accurately portrays the German bomber flying towards Exbury from the Isle of Wight, although its flight across the Solent was direct, and unlike the zigzag path described by the novelist. Lt Craigie, the captain of a tank landing craft, correctly identifies the plane as a Ju 188, and the description of the aircraft being black and twin-engined is also accurate; at least, the underside of the bomber was spray-painted black. The altitude flown by the Junkers across the Solent in the fictional account -1,000ft - is also consistent with official reports of the incident. As the bomber flies up and down the Solent in the novel, Craigie assumes that it is carrying out photo-reconnaissance of the invasion fleet.[8] This was certainly one of the ideas to have emerged in the wake of the real-life incident.

In the story, as Janet Prentice fires at the intruder with an Oerlikon gun, the wheels of the Junkers are lowered. There is much significance in this, as an RAF intelligence officer later points out to her, since lowering the undercarriage of a plane was an internationally-recognised signal of the intention to surrender.[9] In reality, however, there is no evidence that the Exbury Junkers had its wheels down at any stage. Shute modifies the facts here in order to cause Janet Prentice to experience an irrevocable sense of guilt about what she has done.

The novelist also describes other anti-aircraft batteries firing at the bomber, one of which shoots off the tail-fin before the plane dives into the ground.[10] In real life, the shooting down of the Ju 188 was officially credited jointly to Anti-Aircraft Command and to the RAF Typhoons, but there is no mention of the latter in the novel. And, of course, the involvement of a Wren in the destruction of the German bomber is entirely fictitious; simply a scenario designed to conjure up a desperate situation for the central character.

Shute's description of the manner in which the Junkers crashed is not totally accurate. In the fictional account, one of the engines lay at the point where the Ju 188 first hit the ground, before the German plane crashed through a hedge, across a lane, and through a second hedge into the field beyond.[11] In reality, it was the two engines which broke free and crashed through the hedge, crossing the narrow road and rolling into the next field. A small point, certainly, but *aficionados* of *Requiem for a Wren* may find this interesting nonetheless.

One particularly memorable detail in Shute's description of the aftermath of the Junkers crash is the action of a Navy serviceman, a *subaltern*, covering up the bodies of the dead men with two parachutes.[12] This was undoubtedly based on the real-life actions of George James, a telegraphist with Combined Operations Bombardment Unit, who hurriedly covered up some of the bodies as he could see civilians, including children, making their way along the narrow road towards the crash site. On learning that he had been given a cameo role in the novel, George recently commented that *it was nice of Nevil to promote me.*

As mentioned previously, much is made in *Requiem*, as indeed it was in real life, of the fact that the German bomber had been carrying so many men. The view expressed that *they must have been jammed in, sitting on each other's knees* was faithful to the words which the novelist had earlier written in his unpublished Ministry of Information article, when he had mused upon this curious incident in his capacity as a war correspondent.[13] As already explained, whilst it was true that the Ju 188 officially had a crew of four or five, it was apparently possible to accommodate seven men in the cockpit without it being quite as cramped as Shute had imagined. Nevertheless, the image of the cockpit being jam-packed was highly appropriate for the fictional account, given the storyline that the plane was carrying men who had been escaping from the Nazi regime.

In *Requiem*, the novelist describes all the casualties of the Junkers crash as being NCOs, and he refers to them as *either corporals or sergeants.*[14] In real life, four of the seven men were of the *Unteroffizier* rank, equivalent to RAF Corporal, two were *Obergefreiter*, equivalent to the Leading Aircraftman rank, and one was a *Gefreiter*, equivalent to Aircraftman, First Class. When Janet Prentice is summoned to the Captain's office, after she has shot down the Ju 188, she learns from the intelligence officer from nearby Beaulieu aerodrome that the men on board the German bomber were all Poles or Czechs.[15] This crucial element of the story was, of course, inspired by the fact that several of the men killed in the real crash appeared to have Slavonic origins, on the evidence of their identity discs and personal documents found at the scene. Nevil Shute must have been told all about this by the young Air Force officer to whom he spoke at the crash site at Exbury on the morning of 18 April 1944.

The fact that this wartime incident provided Nevil Shute with such lasting inspiration for a novel (remembering that the book was published eleven years after the event) is surely testimony to its truly enigmatic quality. And there can be no doubt that the blurring of fiction and fact in *Requiem for a Wren* has served to romanticise still further the real-life mystery of the Exbury Junkers.

61. Martyn Dryden, a member of the Nevil Shute Norway Foundation, studies his first-edition copy of *Requiem for a Wren* on the lawn in front of Exbury House, which Shute referred to as 'Exbury Hall' in the novel.

62. Some 50 members of the Nevil Shute Norway Foundation visited Exbury during their UK Conference in late June 2003, in order to discover more about the facts behind the fiction.

CHAPTER 8

Unravelling the Threads

It has already been established that the seven men on board the Ju 188 on 18 April 1944 were all regular members of the Luftwaffe, and that there was a perfectly good reason for all seven to have been travelling on that particular aircraft, despite the normal crew complement being just four or five. But this still does not explain how the Junkers came to be flying alone in broad daylight to an area of the Hampshire coast where a huge number of Allied troops and landing craft were massing, in preparation for the Normandy landings.

In the immediate aftermath of the Junkers crash, there were two main schools of thought. Firstly, some believed that the plane had been conducting photo-reconnaissance of the invasion fleet which was building up in the Solent and the Beaulieu river. Secondly, there was speculation that the crew, whatever their origins, may have deliberately flown across the English Channel in order to escape from the Nazi regime.

63. A Junkers Ju 188 E, similar to the one which flew alone in broad daylight into the hornets' nest of the Allied invasion preparations. What was the real reason for this mysterious flight?

Firstly, to examine the reconnaissance theory. At face value, it does seem far too much of a coincidence that this German plane should have flown right into an area of the utmost importance and sensitivity to the Allies. The fact that the Junkers did not drop any bombs (the Air Ministry's investigation confirmed that no bombs had been carried), and that it had circled over the Isle of Wight and Beaulieu river area in a highly-suspicious manner added further weight to the idea that this aircraft had been on a scouting mission.[1]

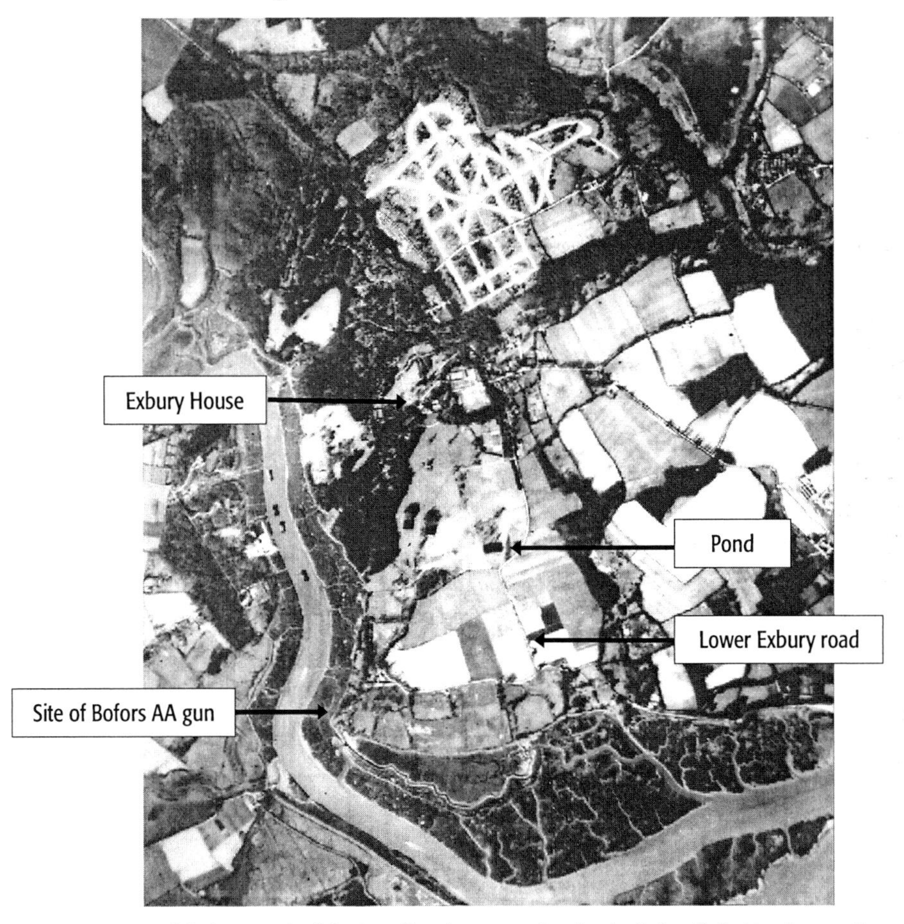

64. An aerial photograph of the Beaulieu river area taken by the Luftwaffe in March 1943. Four vessels can be seen in the river adjacent to the Exbury estate, which is on the east bank. The pond into which the Junkers crashed a year later can also be seen, just to the right of a small wood, and close to a sharp bend in the Lower Exbury road.

However, there was certainly no sign of a camera in the wrecked bomber when it was examined by an RAF intelligence officer; despite the fuselage having been burnt out, there would surely have been some evidence if this had been the case. The official Luftwaffe report into the loss of Ju 188 Z6 EK and its crew stated that the plane had not been engaged in operations against the enemy at the time.[2] This seems to confirm that the Junkers had not officially been tasked with carrying out reconnaissance or any other mission over England that morning. And, besides, reconnaissance was not normally a role performed by 2./KG66, the unit to which the bomber and its crew belonged. The fact that the underside of the Ju 188 had been spray-painted black also confirms that, at that time, it was officially assigned to night operations. This is consistent with what is known about the role of the pathfinder units of I/KG66 in the *Steinbock* reprisal raids.[3] The Junkers would therefore not have been expected to be flying anywhere near enemy territory alone in broad daylight.

As mentioned previously, for some time the Allies had been weaving an elaborate plan of deception, codenamed *Fortitude*, which was designed to fool the Germans into thinking that the main thrust of the invasion would be mounted from south-east England against the Pas de Calais area of the French coast. It was vital, therefore, that no enemy aircraft should have been allowed to carry out detailed reconnaissance of those areas of southern England where the invasion force was actually being assembled. Although a lone hit-and-run raider had occasionally penetrated British air defences, the appearance of a German bomber in broad daylight was something of a rarity at this stage in the war.

It is interesting to note what the Germans were deducing about the Allied invasion plans, at this time, from reconnaissance and other information gathering efforts. By the end of April 1944, just days after the Exbury Junkers crash, German air reconnaissance had discovered substantial concentrations of invasion shipping along the coasts of south-west England. This apparently drew the attention of *Generalfeldmarschall* Gerd von Runstedt, commander of the Western Front, to the possibilities of an Allied assault in the Normandy and Brittany regions.[4] But the area visited by the Ju 188 on 18 April could not be regarded as south-west England, and therefore this reconnaissance report could not have been derived from any radio communication from its crew before the bomber crashed at

Exbury. Moving closer to D-Day, von Runstedt's situation report of 8 May 1944 referred to Allied landing craft concentrations in the area north of the Isle of Wight.[5] Whilst this was precisely the area over which the Ju 188 had flown on 18 April, there are no clues as to how this information had been obtained. If the latter reconnaissance report had been derived from the Junkers flight then its crew would have had to communicate the information to a Luftwaffe ground station before the bomber was brought down on the Hampshire mainland. According to the *RAF Signals Intelligence Service Air Activity Summary* for 18 April 1944, no communications whatsoever were detected from any aircraft of the pathfinder unit I/KG66 during the period in question, which therefore seems to rule out this possibility.[6]

Weighing up all the facts, then, there is no evidence to support the view that Ju 188 Z6 EK had flown to England in order to conduct reconnaissance of the Allied invasion fleet.

Now to consider the second theory about the lone German bomber's flight across the English Channel; namely, that this was an attempted defection which went tragically wrong.

This possibility had been suggested, first and foremost, by the unusually large number of men on board the plane, and the misconception that they would have been packed into the cockpit like sardines. The Slavonic names and/or origins of several of the men served to reinforce the view that this bomber had not been on official Luftwaffe business. Once the details of the strange behaviour of the Junkers before it crashed had also come to light, this merely added to the speculation. In particular, the fact that the plane was circling as if looking for somewhere to land, the firing of red Very lights and its apparent lack of evasive action when under attack; it all seemed to add up.

Having already established that there was nothing sinister about the number of men on board the Ju 188, nor anything mysterious about their identities, it is time to examine the strange behaviour of the German bomber, to determine whether or not this supports the defection theory.

First of all, it is certain that the Junkers was meant to have flown that morning from its rear base at Avord in central France to the advanced airfield at Soesterberg in Holland, to prepare for a pathfinding mission in support of a night raid on London. Another member of the ground crew serving with 2./KG66, who was a good friend of Leonhard Schwingenstein, made the same journey from Avord on board a different Ju 188 that morning, and his plane had taken off at about the same time. According to him, a number of the aircraft of the second *Staffel* of KG66 had flown to Soesterberg that day with ground crew also on board.[7]

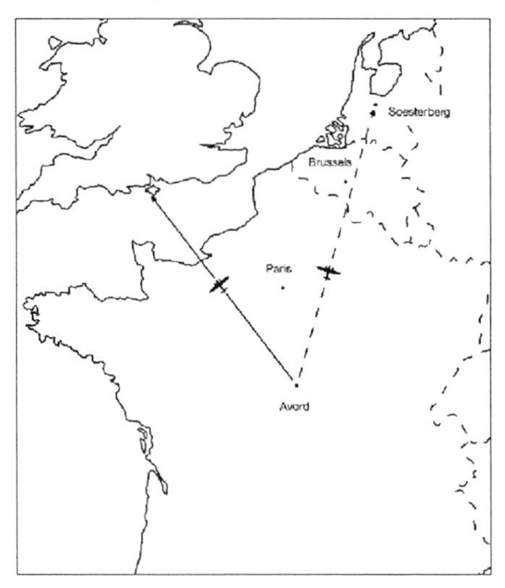

65. The Ju 188 took off from its base at Avord in central France. It should have flown on a north-north-easterly heading to the advanced airfield at Soesterberg in Holland. Why, instead, did it fly in a north-westerly direction across the English Channel directly towards the Isle of Wight and the Hampshire coast?

The distance from Avord to Soesterberg is approximately 370 miles, as the crow flies, and the journey would have involved the Junkers flying in a north-north-easterly direction, on a true bearing of approximately 18°. From Avord to St Catherine's Point on the south coast of the Isle of Wight, the route which the bomber actually took, is about 295 miles and in a north-westerly direction, on a true bearing of about 325°. Thus, the German bomber deviated by roughly 53° from its intended course. Indications are that it did not change direction from taking off at Avord until it reached the south coast of the Isle of Wight. Whatever the intentions of the crew, then, they must have believed that they were on the right heading for their destination up to that point.

When the Ju 188 was first detected by British radar, to the west of Le Havre, it was flying at a height of roughly 600ft.[8] As it continued to fly in a north-westerly direction across the English Channel, it climbed to 4,000ft. By this time, the weather conditions had significantly improved; the rain had died out, the cloud base was much higher, at 1,000 to 2,000ft, and visibility had increased to between three and five miles.[9] So, why did the German bomber climb to a much greater altitude at this point? Was the pilot deliberately keeping the aircraft above the cloud which, by now, was only patchy on this fine spring morning?

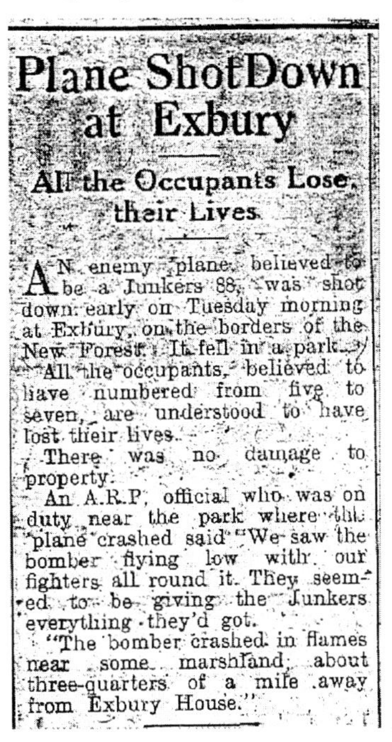

Plane Shot Down at Exbury

All the Occupants Lose their Lives

AN enemy plane, believed to be a Junkers 88, was shot down early on Tuesday morning at Exbury, on the borders of the New Forest. It fell in a park. All the occupants, believed to have numbered from five to seven, are understood to have lost their lives.

There was no damage to property.

An A.R.P. official who was on duty near the park where the plane crashed said "We saw the bomber flying low with our fighters all round it. They seemed to be giving the Junkers everything they'd got.

"The bomber crashed in flames near some marshland, about three-quarters of a mile away from Exbury House."

66. *Isle of Wight County Press*, 22 April 1944 (below).

67. *New Milton and District Advertiser & Lymington Times*, 22 April 1944 (right).

South Coast Air Raids.

Early on Tuesday morning an enemy machine, flying very low in and out of cloud, was hotly assailed by ground defences in a southern district. It cruised around, machine-gunning at times, and was eventually shot down. It was a Junkers 188. Residents in the district, many of whom were brought out of their beds by the air raid siren, saw the machine as it dived out of the clouds and flew very low over the coast, low enough to be engaged by machine-guns, and the gunners did not miss the chance. Its five occupants were killed when the machine crashed.

The fact that the bomber changed direction significantly for the first time as it approached the Isle of Wight coastline suggests that the crew had visual contact with the ground at this point. If they had been on the correct course for Soesterberg, then they would have reached the Antwerp area of Belgium by this time, and there should have been no need for such a change of direction. The subsequent circling over the northern part of the Isle of Wight at low altitude was considered by some to be evidence that the crew were looking for somewhere to land and give themselves up, especially since, at one point, the plane had apparently loitered over the aerodrome at West Cowes. Evidently, at this stage, the Junkers crew were looking for something, but what was it that they were trying to find?

There has been some doubt as to whether the Ju 188 returned fire at any point when it was being attacked either by anti-aircraft guns or the Typhoons, and this has been cited as further evidence that the crew had flown to England without any hostile intent. One of the contemporary newspaper reports of the incident stated that the Junkers had *cruised around, machine-gunning at times.*[10]

The other piece of evidence that the German bomber did use its guns came from one of the RAF Typhoon pilots. In his combat report, F/Lt Vernon Sanders stated that he had *experienced slight return fire* from the Ju 188.[11] However, none of those who observed the Junkers coming under attack from the anti-aircraft guns and the fighters believed that the German plane returned fire. Is it just possible, then, that what Sanders deemed to be *slight return fire* was in fact the red Very lights which were launched from the bomber's cockpit as the Typhoons began their attack?

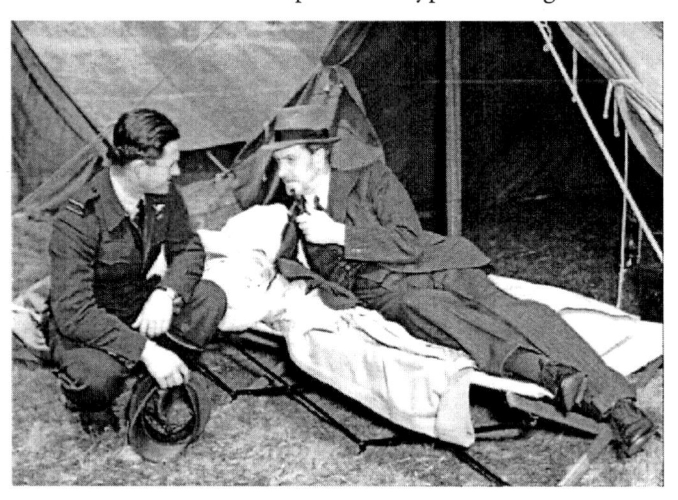

68. F/Lt Vernon Sanders of 266 (Rhodesia) Squadron pictured here having a chat with the Prime Minister of Southern Rhodesia, during the latter's visit to Needs Oar Point on 18 May 1944. This was exactly one month to the day after Sanders and F/Sgt Don Dodd had forced down the Ju 188 at Exbury. In his combat report, Sanders recorded that he had experienced slight return fire from the German bomber.

The RAF investigation into the crashed bomber revealed that its guns had indeed been loaded, and live ammunition could be heard exploding in the wreckage at Exbury for some time after the crash.[12] And several years afterwards Maurice Passingham, who worked on the Exbury estate, came across a German shell in the roadside ditch close to where the plane had come down. But even if the Typhoon pilot's observations were correct, why did the Ju 188 offer only slight return fire? Surely, at this stage, its crew must have known that they were fighting for their lives.

And what can be deduced from the firing of the red Very lights? Those who favoured the defection theory cited this as additional evidence that the crew were trying to signal their non-hostile intentions. As detailed in Chapter 1, several eyewitnesses commented on seeing the red flares. In confirmation of these eyewitness accounts, the Air Ministry report into the Junkers crash mentioned that empty red signal cartridges were found in the wreckage at Exbury.[13]

At the time, it had appeared to Jock Leal at the Royal Observer Corps post on the Isle of Wight that a red Very light had been fired each time that the bomber had made a turn, whilst flying low over the island. However, it is equally possible that the red flares had coincided with the German plane coming under attack from various anti-aircraft batteries and, subsequently, from the RAF Typhoons. It was not unknown for German aircrew to fire coloured flares in an attempt to confuse British air defences and to give themselves time to escape. However, in this instance, the Junkers was flying so low that it could easily be identified as an enemy aircraft, and therefore any attempt to fool the anti-aircraft crews would surely have been pointless.

When asked recently about this use of red Very lights, Helmut Thomale, who had been a radio operator with the same pathfinder unit, commented:

> *When I read that empty red signal cartridges were found in the wreckage, I suspect that the Ju 188 had problems from being attacked and fired off red flares. Red flares meant: 'I have an emergency and need help. I need an emergency landing site.' These flares were fired from a Very pistol, mostly by the observer. Each crew member possessed a Very pistol for the eventuality that he had to bale out over water. In all the*

pockets of my flying combination suit, I carried nothing but red signal cartridges.

But were the crew of Z6 EK genuinely signalling that they had no hostile intentions, and that they wanted to land? If it had truly been the men's objective to fly across to England to give themselves up, then surely the pilot would have signalled this by lowering the plane's undercarriage. After all, this was the recognised signal of surrender, as Nevil Shute had accurately reflected in *Requiem for a Wren*. Moreover, if the crew had planned to defect, would they really have chosen to fly to the south coast of England, where they might have known that they would be in for a hot reception? It seems doubtful, to say the least.

According to Helmut Thomale, morale in the pathfinder *Staffeln* of I/KG66 was extremely high in the early part of 1944. Other veterans of I/KG66 have also testified to its exemplary spirit, even at this stage of the war when the Luftwaffe was becoming badly depleted. Most importantly, on the evidence of available information about four of the seven men on board the Exbury Junkers, it seems impossible that any of them would have chosen to desert. There can be no doubt that they all shared a very firm sense of duty, a devout belief in the German cause, and unbreakable family ties. This makes the defection theory very unlikely indeed.

So, if the Ju 188 was not on a reconnaissance mission and its crew were not intending to defect, what could have been the reason for the German bomber's peculiar appearance over this part of southern England in broad daylight, just seven weeks before D-Day?

It seems that there is just one other possibility to consider. Could it be that the strange behaviour of the Junkers before it was forced down at Exbury was due simply to the fact that its crew had completely lost their bearings and flown unintentionally into the Allied invasion preparations? At face value, this scenario is implausible. After all, how on earth could an aircraft from a specialist pathfinder unit have strayed so wildly off course?

Leonhard Schwingenstein's ground crew friend, who made the same journey on board a different Ju 188 that morning, recalls that weather conditions were extremely poor over France and Belgium *en route* to Soesterberg. Not only was there rain, low cloud and poor visibility at

Avord but a heavy ground mist was also encountered at some stage. According to other KG66 veterans, fog could develop quite fast and unexpectedly in the Avord region. The Ju 188 on which Schwingenstein's friend was travelling apparently encountered such thick fog at one stage that the pilot had to circle close to the ground in order for the crew to get their bearings, such was their concern that they may have become lost in the bad weather. In fact, they were near Brussels by that time and, therefore, still very much on course, and they eventually reached their destination in Holland without further difficulty. The ground mechanic remembers to this day waiting in vain at Soesterberg for Leonhard Schwingenstein to arrive. He is convinced that the aircraft on which his friend was travelling must have become hopelessly lost in the poor weather which had almost proved his own downfall.[14]

However, there is a significant difference here, since the doomed Ju 188 seems to have flown off course right from the moment that it took off from Avord. True, the poor visibility and low cloud over much of France would not have helped the crew to spot their predicament, but surely something else altogether must have been responsible for the initial, catastrophic deviation, if this theory is correct.

69. How could the specialist pathfinder crew have set off from Avord in completely the wrong direction?

Of course, there were numerous instances during the war of both Allied and German aircraft becoming hopelessly lost. Indeed, it was not unprecedented for German crews to land in Britain by mistake, having become completely disorientated as a result of bad weather or encounters with Allied aircraft. In some cases, the German planes had been victims of 'meaconing', which was a deception measure practised by the RAF's 80 (Signals) Wing. This technique involved a British radio-relay station receiving the signal transmitted by a German navigational beacon, and then re-transmitting it on the same radio frequency. The German aircraft using the beacon would then receive a faulty bearing. The degree of error depended on its distance from the German beacon and the British 'meacon'; the nearer the aircraft was to the 'meacon' then the greater the error would be.[15]

One instance of 'meaconing' involved a Dornier Do 217 bomber taking a bearing on a beacon at Paimpol in Brittany. The crew subsequently saw the coastline below them and assumed this to be the northern coast of the Brest peninsula. Their direction-finding equipment indicated that their course was correct. However, by this time, they were actually near Ilfracombe in Devon. The Paimpol beacon was being 'meaconed' by a British transmitter in the West Country (near Templecombe), and when the Dornier reached this location, it circled around the area of the transmitter, with the crew totally confused as to their whereabouts.[16]

Tempting though it might be to attribute the strange behaviour of the lone Junkers on 18 April 1944 to 'meaconing', there does not appear to have been a 'meacon' transmitter located on the Isle of Wight, nor along the part of the Hampshire coast between the Beaulieu river and Southampton Water. There must have been another reason, then, for the aircraft having set off in completely the wrong direction from its base in central France.

Helmut Thomale, the Ju 188 radio operator who also served with 2./KG66, suspects that the key to this whole mystery lay with the German bomber's master compass. The observer seems to have been far too experienced to have made a fundamental mistake when calculating the course to take from Avord to Soesterberg. However, if the compass itself had been faulty, then this might just explain why the crew of Ju 188 Z6 EK had set off in the wrong direction.

Assuming this is actually what happened, then the poor visibility over much of France that morning would certainly have compounded the problem. It can only be assumed that, as the Junkers crossed the English Channel and approached the Isle of Wight, visibility had at last become good enough for the crew to become suspicious of their whereabouts.

If the faulty navigation theory is correct, then the loitering over the Isle of Wight at low level was presumably an attempt by the pilot and observer to get their bearings, just as the other Ju 188 *en route* to Soesterberg had circled low over the Brussels area. Moreover, in firing the red Very lights, the crew may simply have been trying to placate what they initially believed to be friendly anti-aircraft fire. It is impossible to know at what stage the awful reality of their position would have dawned on the Junkers crew, but by the time they were pounced on by the RAF Typhoons they must surely have realised their predicament.

Perhaps the lack of return fire from the Junkers when being attacked by the Typhoons, and the firing of the red Very lights in those final few minutes over the Hampshire mainland, was a desperate signal that the crew wanted to get the plane down safely, having realised the hopelessness of their position. If so, then this signal sadly went unnoticed.

And, lastly, what about the white material, possibly clothing or a parachute, which an eyewitness had noticed hanging outside the crew compartment as the bomber had just cleared the rooftops in Exbury village? Was this simply as a result of the cockpit canopy having been badly holed, or could it have been a deliberate last-ditch attempt by the crew to signal to their assailants that they knew the game was up, and that they wanted to land. Either way, the tragic finale could not be averted; the fate of the Junkers crew had been sealed.

70. The Junkers passed so low over Exbury village that at least one crew member could be seen in the front of the cockpit. But what was the significance of the white material which was seen draped outside the crew compartment? Was this a final, desperate signal which sadly went unnoticed?

CHAPTER 9

A Few Loose Ends

It is likely, then, that Ju 188 Z6 EK stumbled upon the Allies' invasion preparations completely by accident on 18 April 1944 because of a compass malfunction, which had caused it to stray wildly off course. The strange behaviour of the German bomber probably reflected the fact that the crew were confused as to their whereabouts and then, finally realising the hopelessness of their situation, desperately tried to find somewhere to put down safely. Whilst this is the probable explanation for the bizarre behaviour of the lone Junkers, there remain several loose ends which stubbornly refuse to be tied.

Firstly, there is the information about the incoming Ju 188 which had been received in the Royal Observer Corps Operations Room in Winchester early that morning. The approach of the German bomber was apparently known about in advance, and *no offensive action was going to be taken*. However, in that case, why were none of the anti-aircraft sites on the Isle of Wight and on the Hampshire mainland instructed not to engage the incoming Junkers? And what kind of information could have been received in advance to warrant no offensive action being taken against the enemy aircraft, which was heading straight for highly-sensitive military locations? One can only speculate about this.

Secondly, in the words of Helmut Thomale, the former radio operator from the same pathfinder unit, *where were the English fighters?* After all, the Junkers had first been detected heading towards Britain at 7.04am, and yet it was not intercepted by the Typhoons of 266 Squadron until after 7.30am. Even then, F/Lt Sanders's combat report clearly states that the German bomber was spotted purely by chance as the RAF pilots were returning to Needs Oar Point airfield. There is no indication whatsoever that Sanders had been alerted over his radio to the presence of the enemy aircraft.[1] As previously mentioned, RAF records state that fighters from several other squadrons were also detailed to intercept the German bomber, and yet there is no evidence that any other RAF planes confronted the incoming enemy aircraft.[2]

71. Pilots of 266 (Rhodesia) Squadron pictured in 1945. Their CO at the time was S/Ldr Ronnie Sheward DFC (seated third from left). Third from right is F/Lt David Hughes DFC, who was in the section of four aircraft returning to Needs Oar Point when the Ju 188 was spotted on the morning of 18 April 1944.

With preparations for the Normandy landings in full swing, and this part of southern England consequently being on the highest state of alert, it does seem rather puzzling that the Junkers was able to circle over the Isle of Wight and to fly across the Solent before being forced down. Admittedly, however, its low altitude must have made it a relatively difficult target to hit for the various anti-aircraft sites which attempted to engage the early morning intruder.

72/73. Remains of the anti-aircraft site at Lower Exbury which fired at, and reportedly hit, the German bomber.

74. Looking south from the site of the Bofors gun at Lower Exbury towards the entrance to the Beaulieu river. The Ju 188 came from this direction and must have flown almost directly overhead. If no offensive action was meant to be taken against the incoming German bomber, why was this not communicated to the anti-aircraft sites?

It also seems somewhat peculiar that the Junkers crew had not spotted that they were flying such a long distance over water as they crossed the English Channel. After all, visibility had significantly improved, to between three and five miles, and the cloud base was now up to between 1,000 and 2,000ft. This also begs the question as to why the German bomber had climbed from 600 to 4,000ft as it left the French coast behind. At face value, it would appear the pilot was deliberately trying to keep the plane above the cloud cover at this time. But why should this have been necessary if the crew had believed they were flying over friendly territory?

Finally, Helmut Thomale points out that it should still have been possible for the Ju 188 crew to get a fix on their position, even if they had lost their way and had no visual contact with the ground. Each plane had direction-finding equipment on board, which was used to get a bearing on a radio transmitter or beacon. Using the Long Wave radio equipment, it was possible to pick up an approach beam from Soesterberg. In Belgium, Holland and northern France, there were many ground stations to aid navigation.

The RAF technical inspection of the Exbury Junkers confirmed the presence of a Long Wave radio incorporating direction-finding equipment. Furthermore, for some reason, rather than the observer and the radio operator sharing a single DF receiver, on this particular aircraft an additional receiver had been installed.[3]

What were the chances of the direction-finding equipment and the compass having developed a fault on the same flight? Highly unlikely, according to Helmut Thomale, who recalls that the equipment on board the Ju 188s of 2./KG66 was invariably well-maintained.

And so this investigation draws to a close, ending in probability and likelihood, but with several key questions unresolved, and the mystery of the Exbury Junkers still very much alive. It looks as if Nevil Shute was right when he wrote in 1944 about this *enigma of a curious war...*

Perhaps we never shall hear all the answers.[4]

CHAPTER 10

Reflections

Sixty years on, the Junkers crash at Exbury continues to leave its mark. Whilst the pond in which the German bomber came to grief was drained many years ago, this patch of land in the field to the south of Exbury House remains quite distinct. The ground is very soft underfoot and has been left uncultivated, and the rushes which fringed the pond still grow there. Furthermore, two thinner areas of the hedge bordering the narrow Lower Exbury road still mark the places where the engines of the Ju 188 went crashing through, narrowly missing Leading Seaman Reg 'Tug' Wilson as he cycled past.

75. The exact spot where the Junkers crashed (looking north).
The site of the pond is very distinct, even today.

76. The site of the crash (looking south). The thinner area of hedge still marks where one of the bomber's engines went crashing through.

77. November 2000: A period of heavy rain turned this part of the field into a swamp, evoking memories of that fateful morning in April 1944, when the Ju 188 came to a violent end in the shallow pond.

Although the wreckage of the German bomber was taken away on the day of the crash, not surprisingly some parts had been left embedded in the boggy ground in which the pond lay. Margaret Mead was a Wren at HMS Mastodon at the time. When out walking her dog in the field several years later, the dog emerged from the water with a small light-blue, metallic object which had obviously been a part of the aircraft. More pieces of the bomber were unearthed several years ago when the site was scoured extensively with a metal detector.

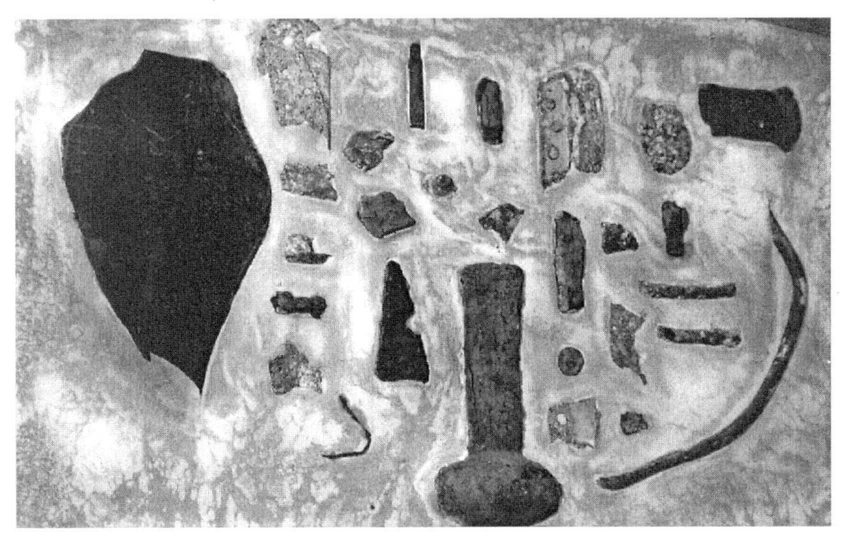

78. Parts of the bomber unearthed by a metal detector included a wheel hub, some piping from one of the engines, shell casing from a machine-gun, several pieces of melted alloy and a piece of rubber sheeting, possibly from an inner tube. Two bullets fired from the Typhoons' cannons were also found. These items were mounted as one of a number of exhibits displayed at Exbury in 1994 to commemorate the 50th Anniversary of D-Day.

The large field into which the Ju 188's engines had rolled has also been the subject of some interest over the years. Several local people, who had witnessed the events at Exbury, had been convinced that the pilot was aiming to land the Junkers on this flat, wide-open stretch of land, and would have succeeded in doing so had the badly-damaged bomber not encountered the pond before the narrow road. Curiously, some 10 years earlier, the same field had been used as a landing site for a De Havilland Dragon of the King's Flight, when the Prince of Wales had visited the Rothschilds at Exbury House.

79. A De Havilland Dragon carrying the Prince of Wales comes into land across the Lower Exbury road. The copse next to the pond where the Ju 188 was to crash some 10 years later can just be made out in the distance on the right hand side.

80. Edward, Prince of Wales, pictured with Mrs Lionel de Rothschild in the Lower Exbury road during his visit in May 1934.

81. The De Havilland Dragon, which brought the Prince of Wales to Exbury, landed in the large field just south of the site where the German bomber was to come down 10 years later. Several local people were convinced that the Junkers pilot had been aiming to land his aircraft in the same spot.

The Junkers episode has certainly touched the lives of a number of those people who played a part in it. Many of the former servicemen at HMS Mastodon have commented that they will never forget the scene of total devastation which they witnessed at the crash site, and which brought home to them in graphic detail the human tragedy of war. Several others recall how they visited the graves of the young Germans at Fawley, in some cases years after the crash. This says something about the impression left by this wartime incident, bearing in mind that it happened only weeks before a number of the men at Mastodon took part in D-Day, and encountered scenes on the Normandy beaches and beyond which they would never forget.

James Kyle, a Typhoon pilot with 197 Squadron, had been to see the wrecked bomber that morning, along with those pilots of 266 Squadron who had forced down the German plane:

> *I had never witnessed such a mass of destruction, death and damage at close range. We stood speechless, nothing hostile in our shared silence, gazing at the appalling sight.*[1]

82. James Kyle DFM, a Typhoon pilot with 197 Squadron.

He still remembers this having been a most sobering experience.

The sad sight of the fair-haired, blue-eyed young German airman, who was being cared for in the sick bay at HMS Mastodon, had also prompted a Wren to wonder, *What are we all fighting for? It seems so futile.* And then there were the women and children of Fawley, who had lined the route as the funeral procession had made its way to the church, *full of sorrow and sympathy for the German mothers and families* and all feeling the *utter futility of war.*

The Land Girls still vividly remember the harrowing day when they witnessed not only the downing of the German bomber but also the death of the young British pilot when his light aircraft hit the ground and burst into flames. Joan McCluskey (Bunty Cooper) has remarked that this was one of the most horrific days of her life.

83. Nancy Hardy (née Jones), sitting, centre, and Marjorie Maidment (née Pinnock), sitting, left, pictured with other Land Girls in the garden of their hostel in Beaulieu. 18 April 1944 is forever etched in their memory.

84. Joan McCluskey (née Cooper) on the left.

Such has been the fascination with the events of 18 April 1944 at Exbury that some people have linked the crash of the light aircraft directly to that of the Junkers. It has been suggested that the Auster pilot had been part of the team sent to Exbury to investigate the downed German bomber. In some quarters, the story goes that the pilot had collected papers found in the wreckage, and possibly even parts of the Ju 188, and that the weight of the latter had been responsible for the plane's demise.

The truth is that the Auster crash at Exbury had no connection whatsoever with the German bomber. Its pilot was 25-year-old Hugh Evans, a Captain in the Royal Artillery, who was serving with RAF Air Observation Post 661 Squadron.[2] AOP squadrons were formed during the Second World War to control artillery fire and to carry out aerial observation in support of ground troops. Using their slow speed and agility to avoid enemy planes, AOP aircraft operated from fields close to the ground forces which they were supporting. On the day of the crash at Exbury, Captain Evans had been training with an Army unit in preparation for the ground advance in the Normandy countryside. Thus, the loss of the observation plane and its pilot was, quite simply, a tragic coincidence.

What became of the Typhoon pilots who had forced down the Ju 188? Mac McMurdon, who served with 266 (Rhodesia) Squadron and is now a farmer in trouble-torn Zimbabwe, remembers that Vernon Sanders and Don Dodd had been badly affected by rumours that the Junkers crew had flown across to England to give themselves up. But this all changed when the squadron later received a visit from an Air Ministry official, who had come to say that the pilots had been right to shoot down the German bomber and that they had been acting under orders. Sanders went on to be awarded the DFC in October 1944, and he survived the war. He is thought to have died in approximately 1990. Don Dodd, then a Flying Officer, was shot down near the Dutch/German border during an armed reconnaissance mission in April 1945, and was briefly taken prisoner of war. He was awarded the *Croix de Guerre*. He too survived the war and lived for many years in South Africa. He is believed to have died during the 1990s.

The whereabouts of the Iron Cross, which had been taken from one of the Ju 188's crew at Exbury, has remained something of a mystery until fairly recently. It transpired that the sailor from HMS Mastodon, who originally took the medal, had left it along with other 'souvenirs' in the safekeeping of a local lady, Mrs Barker – the mother of Maurice Barker, the aircraft engine inspector. Maurice had an abiding memory of his mother, having spoken to the sailor on the doorstep of their home in Exbury, entering the room with a Belgian Browning and an ammunition belt in her hands. This had caused great amusement within the family since his mother was a pillar of the Blackfield Baptist chapel.

85. Mrs Barker, a pillar of the Baptist chapel, returned from the front door holding a Belgian Browning.

When the sailor came to collect his booty, he let the Barkers keep the Iron Cross. Years later, the medal was passed on to Reg Wheeler, the local butcher's roundsman, who collected memorabilia. It remained in his possession until about 1958 when it became known that the mother of one of the young airmen killed in the Junkers crash was coming to visit his grave at Fawley. Confirming that her son had indeed been awarded an Iron Cross, the German lady was handed the medal.

Of course, it was the families of the Junkers crew on whom the impact of this wartime event was the most profound. Initially, they received the standard, brief notification that their loved ones had been killed, and their personal effects were duly returned. Official confirmation of their death and burial was received after the war, as were photographs of the graves at Fawley. But no real explanation was ever provided as to what had happened to the seven young men on 18 April 1944. Certainly, no more information was forthcoming than that contained in the Luftwaffe's official report into the loss of the aircraft and its crew, which had simply stated that the cause of this incident was unknown.

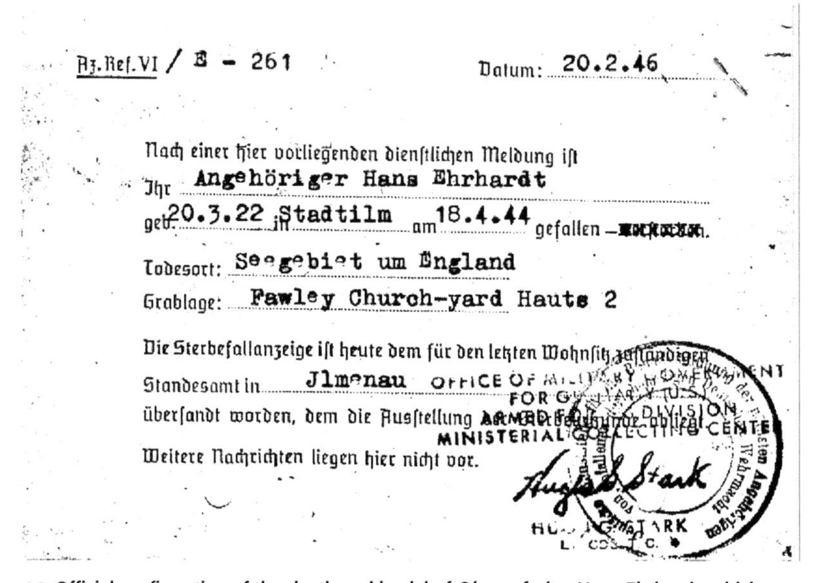

Az.Ref.VI / B - 261 Datum: 20.2.46

Nach einer hier vorliegenden dienstlichen Meldung ist
Ihr Angehöriger Hans Ehrhardt
geb. 20.3.22 in Stadtilm am 18.4.44 gefallen –
Todesort: Seegebiet um England
Grablage: Fawley Church-yard Hauts 2

Die Sterbefallanzeige ist heute dem für den letzten Wohnsitz zuständigen
Standesamt in Jlmenau
übersandt worden, dem die Ausstellung der Sterbeurkunde obliegt.
Weitere Nachrichten liegen hier nicht vor.

OFFICE OF MILITARY GOVERNMENT
FOR GERMANY (U.S.)
ARMED FORCES DIVISION
MINISTERIAL COLLECTING CENTER

86. Official confirmation of the death and burial of *Obergefreiter* Hans Ehrhardt, which was sent to his wife, Elfriede, in early 1946.

The bodies of the seven young men who perished on the Exbury estate were moved from Fawley churchyard and re-interred at the German Military Cemetery (*Deutscher Soldatenfriedhof*) on Cannock Chase in February 1963. This cemetery was built in the early 1960s by the German War Graves Commission, and most of the German servicemen who died in the United Kingdom in both World Wars are now buried there. The cemetery, which is situated in a gentle valley, is bordered to the south by a pine forest. The graves are marked by headstones of Belgian granite, upon which are engraved the names and the dates of birth and death of the 5,000 or so men who lie there. The heather, which is planted along the rows of graves, produces a striking carpet of purple in the summer months.[3]

87. All Saints Church, Fawley, where the seven were initially laid to rest.

88. The German Military Cemetery on Cannock Chase.

89. The plot where the seven young casualties of the Ju 188 crash were finally laid to rest.

90-92. The granite headstones marking the final resting place of Hans Czipin, Robert Schultes, Edgar Vester, Hans Ehrhardt, Eitel Wysotzki and Johann Krause.

93. Hans Schwingenstein visited his cousin Leonhard's grave in 1979.

94. Edmund de Rothschild planted an oak tree at the entrance to Exbury Gardens on Remembrance Sunday in November 2000, in memory of those servicemen stationed at HMS Mastodon who died in the last war.

It is a very moving experience to hear the names of the seven young Luftwaffe members being read out alongside those of British servicemen, at the Remembrance Sunday Service held at St Katharine's Parish Church in the village of Exbury each November. The Exbury Veterans Association, whose President is Edmund de Rothschild, is proud of its connection with the German bomber, and determined that the memory of the young men who came to grief on the Exbury estate should continue to be honoured. Today, Exbury is, of course, best known for its beautiful public gardens, and particularly for its splendid rhododendrons and azaleas.

95. Exbury House, owned by the Rothschild family, is most famous today for its beautiful public gardens, on the east bank of the Beaulieu river.

96. A plaque is mounted at the foot of the flagpole commemorating Exbury House's associations with the Royal Navy between 1942 and 1955. The Exbury Veterans Association keeps this rich tradition alive.

In August 2002, former Marine John Lambourne returned to the crash site at Exbury for the first time since the fateful day in 1944. His memories of that traumatic April morning remain vivid to this day, particularly his encounter with the young airman whom he found, barely alive, lying beneath the hedge. Shortly after the Junkers crash, John went on to experience the horrors of Omaha beach, since he was one of several British Marines who were tasked with supporting the American landings in Normandy.

97. John Lambourne re-visits the exact spot in front of the hedge where he tended one of the young German airmen. John still has a vivid recollection of the demise of the German bomber and the scene which confronted him on reaching the crash site.

The final reflection on this wartime episode comes from Helmut Thomale, who served with the same pathfinder unit as the men who lost their lives on 18 April 1944. On hearing how the people of Exbury remember the young Luftwaffe airmen along with fallen British servicemen, he recently commented:

> *Thank God we have learned in the past 50 years that war is the biggest tragedy for us all.*

When all is said and done, the Exbury Junkers mystery can be regarded as just one of countless wartime incidents whose circumstances have never been fully explained, and perhaps never will be. At the same time, the fact that it has captured the imagination of so many people over the years makes it quite remarkable. This is more than just a curious wartime tale. It is also a very poignant reminder of the fragility of human life amidst the hazards of war. Back in April 1944, with D-Day preparations in their final stages, secrecy was of paramount importance to the Allies, and no risk whatsoever could have been taken with a German bomber flying low over such sensitive military locations. Nevertheless, a thought should surely be spared for the seven young men who climbed on board the Junkers at daybreak on 18 April 1944. They could not have had any idea of the fate that awaited them.

NOTES

CHAPTER 1: Early Morning Intruder

1. At 4am, in the Bourges area, the weather conditions were reported as follows: persistent rain, overcast skies and a cloud base probably around 600 to 1,200ft. Visibility may have been one to two miles, accompanied by a moderate-to-fresh northerly wind. (National Meteorological Archive, Meteorological Office, Bracknell.)
2. AIR 25/209, PRO: 11 Group Ops Activity Synopsis – Appendix to Ops Record Book.
3. On the French coast there was an improvement in conditions: the rain was dying out, the cloud base was higher (1,000 - 2,000ft), surface visibility had increased to between three and five miles, and the surface wind was lighter. (National Meteorological Archive, Meteorological Office, Bracknell.)
4. AIR 40/2417, PRO: ADI(K) Report No 170/1944 of 19 April 1944.
5. *Air War over the Isle of Wight*, H J T Leal, Isle of Wight County Press, 1982, p. 34.
6. AIR 25/209, PRO: 11 Group Ops Activity Synopsis – Appendix to Ops Record Book;

   AIR 40/2417, PRO: ADI(K) Report No 170/1944 of 19 April 1944;

   Air War over the Isle of Wight, H J T Leal, Isle of Wight County Press, 1982, p. 34.
7. *Battles in the Skies over the Isle of Wight*, H J T Leal, Isle of Wight County Press, 1988, reprinted 1993, p. 70.
8. *Ibid.*, p. 7.
9. *Ibid.*, pp. 70-71.
10. National Meteorological Archive, Meteorological Office, Bracknell.
11. AIR 50/105, PRO: Personal Combat Report, F/Lt A V Sanders, 266 Squadron;

    AIR 27/1559, PRO: Ops Record, 266 Squadron;

    AIR 25/209, PRO: 11 Group Ops Activity Synopsis – Appendix to Ops Record Book.
12. AIR 50/105, PRO: Personal Combat Report, F/Lt A V Sanders, 266 Squadron;

    AIR 27/1559, PRO: Ops Record, 266 Squadron;

    AIR 25/209, PRO: 11 Group Ops Activity Synopsis – Appendix to Ops Record Book.

    In his personal combat report, F/Lt Sanders stated that he was *returning from a sortie in 'Exercise Smash'*. The 11 Group Ops Activity Synopsis for 18 April 1944 reported that the exercise involved 26 patrols of 243 aircraft between 6.52am and 9.20pm, and this suggests that *'Smash'* comprised fighter sweeps over the English Channel. However, two former Typhoon pilots from 266 Squadron have independently recalled that, when Sanders spotted the Ju 188, his section of Typhoons was returning to base after carrying out air-to-sea firing practice against a raft anchored in the English Channel. Both sources remember that the Typhoons' cannons had specifically been loaded with ball, rather than the usual high-explosive, armour-piercing, ammunition for this training exercise.

13. AIR 50/105, PRO: Personal Combat Report, F/Lt A V Sanders, 266 Squadron.

CHAPTER 2: Crash and Aftermath

1. Force J was the formation tasked with attacking the Juno sector of the Normandy beaches on D-Day.
2. AIR 50/105, PRO: Personal Combat Report, F/Lt A V Sanders, 266 Squadron.
3. *Air War over the Isle of Wight*, H J T Leal, Isle of Wight County Press, 1982, p. 35.
4. *Typhoon Tale*, James Kyle, GM, 1989, p. 153.
5. Memorial Records, Museum of Army Flying.

CHAPTER 3: Investigation and Speculation

1. AIR 16/173, PRO: Anti-Aircraft Operations against Enemy Aircraft, 18 April 1944;

   AIR 16/962, PRO: Combats and Casualties Report for 18 April 1944 also refers.
2. AIR 40/45, PRO: ADI(G) Report Serial No 234 (Report No 8/106) of 22 April 1944.
3. AIR 25/209, PRO: 11 Group Operations Activity Synopsis – Appendix to Ops Record Book.
4. AIR 40/45, PRO: ADI(G) Report Serial No 234 (Report No 8/106) of 22 April 1944;

   AIR 40/2417, PRO: ADI (K) Report No 170/1944 of 19 April 1944.
5. A *Kampfgeschwader* was roughly equivalent to an RAF bomber group. Each *Geschwader* comprised some 90 aircraft organised into three *Gruppen* (loosely equivalent to RAF wings). Each *Gruppe* was, in turn, organised into three *Staffeln* (similar to RAF squadrons). Individual *Staffeln* were designated with Arabic numerals; hence, in this case, the second squadron of *Kampfgeschwader 66* was designated 2./KG66. *Gruppen* were designated using Roman numerals; hence the first three squadrons of KG66 belonged to I/KG66.
6. AIR 50/105, PRO: Personal Combat Report, F/Lt A V Sanders, 266 Squadron.
7. *Air War over the Isle of Wight*, H J T Leal, Isle of Wight County Press, 1982, p. 35.

CHAPTER 4: The Mystery of the Seven Men

1. Sudetenland was the border area of Czechoslovakia, inhabited mainly by people of German origin, which had been ceded to Germany in 1938. Austria had also been

proclaimed a part of the German Reich in 1938. Whilst East Prussia was already part of Germany, between the First and Second World Wars it had been separated from the rest of the country by the Polish Corridor and the Free City of Danzig.

2. *Namentliche Verlustmeldung, No 21/44*, Bundesarchiv-Militärarchiv, Freiburg;

   Extract from *Verlustfilm 96/10*, Bundesarchiv, Aachen.

3. At this stage of the war, the role of the *Beobachter* was similar to that of an RAF bomber navigator.

4. *Namentliche Verlustmeldung, No 21/44*, Bundesarchiv-Militärarchiv, Freiburg;

   Namentliche Verlustliste, Kampfgeschwader 26, 1939-1945, O IV 72, Bundesarchiv-Militärarchiv, Freiburg;

   Extract from *Bordfilm 150/52*, Bundesarchiv, Aachen.

5. *Namentliche Verlustmeldung, No 21/44*, Bundesarchiv-Militärarchiv, Freiburg;

   Extract from *Bordfilm 163/93*, Bundesarchiv, Aachen.

6. *Namentliche Verlustmeldung, No 21/44*, Bundesarchiv-Militärarchiv, Freiburg;

   Extract from *Bordfilm 169/108*, Bundesarchiv, Aachen.

7. Information provided by Karin Oschmann;

   Namentliche Verlustmeldung, No 21/44, Bundesarchiv-Militärarchiv, Freiburg.

8. *Ibid*;

   Extracts from *Bordfilm 139/20* and from Hans Ehrhardt's *Wehrstammbuch*, Bundesarchiv, Aachen.

9. *Ibid.*

10. Information provided by Maria and Hans Otto;

    Namentliche Verlustmeldung, No 21/44, Bundesarchiv-Militärarchiv, Freiburg.

11. *Ibid.*

12. *Ibid.*

13. *Namentliche Verlustmeldung, No 21/44*, Bundesarchiv-Militärarchiv, Freiburg;

    Extracts from Edgar Vester's *Wehrstammbuch* and *Wehrpaß*, Bundesarchiv, Aachen.

14. Information provided by Dr. Volker Scholz;

    Extracts from Edgar Vester's *Wehrstammbuch* and *Wehrpaß*, Bundesarchiv, Aachen.

15. *Ibid.*

16. *Ibid.*

17. *Verluste I/KG66*, RL 10/638, Bundesarchiv-Militärarchiv, Freiburg.

18. Four of the men held the rank of *Unteroffizier* (roughly equivalent to RAF Corporal), two were of the *Obergefreiter* rank (similar to RAF Leading Aircraftman) and one was a *Gefreiter* (Aircraftman First Class).

19. *Verluste I/KG66,* RL 10/638, Bundesarchiv-Militärarchiv, Freiburg.

20. *Kampfgeschwader 6*, RL 10/564, Bundesarchiv-Militärarchiv, Freiburg.
21. AIR 40/2417, PRO: ADI(K) Report No 170/1944 of 19 April 1944.
22. *Namentliche Verlustliste, Kampfgeschwader 26, 1939-1945*, O IV 72, Bundesarchiv-Militärarchiv, Freiburg;

    Extract from *Bordfilm 150/52*, Bundesarchiv, Aachen.
23. *The Blitz, Then and Now, Volume 3*, Battle of Britain Prints International Ltd, 1990, pp. 328-364.
24. *Verluste I/KG66*, RL 10/638, Bundesarchiv-Militärarchiv, Freiburg.
25. AIR 40/2417, PRO: ADI(K) Report No 170/1944 of 19 April 1944.
26. *Ibid.*
27. *Requiem for a Wren*, Nevil Shute, William Heinemann Ltd, 1955, p. 111.
28. AIR 40/1166, PRO: Air Technical Intelligence Items. This document refers to the use of a three-man container for the packaged delivery, by parachute, of enemy agents or saboteurs. The containers could be fitted to the external bomb racks of several German bomber types, including the Ju 188.

CHAPTER 5: The Luftwaffe Perspective

1. AIR 40/173, PRO: The Junkers 188.
2. *The Blitz: Then and Now, Volume 3*, Battle of Britain Prints Intl. Ltd, 1990, p. 300.
3. *I/KG66 Einsatz England 1943-44*, Lt H Hebestreit, RL 10/638, Bundesarchiv-Militärarchiv, Freiburg;

   Einsatz gegen England 1943-1944, RL 8/65, Bundesarchiv-Militärarchiv, Freiburg.
4. *I/KG66 Einsatz England 1943-44*, Lt H Hebestreit, RL 10/638, Bundesarchiv-Militärarchiv, Freiburg.
5. *Ibid.*
6. *Blitz on Britain*, Alfred Price, Sutton Publishing Ltd, 2000, pp. 180-181.
7. *I/KG66 Einsatz England 1943-44*, Lt H Hebestreit, RL 10/638, Bundesarchiv-Militärarchiv, Freiburg.
8. *Blitz on Britain*, Alfred Price, Sutton Publishing Ltd, 2000, p. 181.
9. *I/KG66 Einsatz England 1943-44*, Lt H Hans Hebestreit, RL 10/638, Bundesarchiv-Militärarchiv, Freiburg.
10. AIR 40/2417, PRO: ADI(K) Report No 170/1944 of 19 April 1944.
11. *Ibid.*
12. *The Blitz, Then and Now, Volume 3*, Battle of Britain Prints Intl. Ltd, 1990, p. 314.
13. *Ibid.*, p. 315.
14. *Ibid.*, pp. 318-327.
15. *Ibid.*, p. 363.

CHAPTER 6: Into the Hornets' Nest

1. *The Beaulieu River Goes To War,* Cyril Cunningham, Montagu Ventures Ltd, 1994, p. 27.
2. *Ibid.*, p. 10, pp. 17-18.
3. *A Short History of HMS Mastodon,* Cyril Cunningham, 1992, pp. 1-4.
4. *Code Name Mulberry: The Planning, Building and Operation of the Normandy Harbours,* Guy Hartcup, David & Charles, 1977, p. 96.
5. *Twelve Airfields,* Alan Brown, 1997.
6. *Ibid.*

CHAPTER 7: The Blurring of Fiction and Fact

1. *Nevil Shute,* Julian Smith, Twayne Publishers, 1976, p. 119. Reprinted by The Paper Tiger, Cresskill, NJ, 2002.
2. *Ibid.*, p. 55.
3. *The Beaulieu River Goes To War,* Cyril Cunningham, Montagu Ventures Ltd, 1994, pp. 40-43.
4. *Second Front – III,* Nevil Shute, Ministry of Information article, 1944.
5. *Ibid.*
6. *Nevil Shute,* Julian Smith, Twayne Publishers, 1976, p. 119. Reprinted by The Paper Tiger, Cresskill, NJ, 2002.
7. *Requiem for a Wren,* Nevil Shute, William Heinemann Ltd, 1955, p. 106.
8. *Ibid.*, p. 108.
9. *Ibid.*, p. 113.
10. *Ibid.*, p. 109.
11. *Ibid.*, p. 110.
12. *Ibid.*, p. 111.
13. *Ibid.*, p. 111, and *Second Front – III,* Nevil Shute, Ministry of Information article, 1944.
14. *Ibid.*, p. 111.
15. *Ibid.*, p. 114.

CHAPTER 8: Unravelling the Threads

1. AIR 40/45, PRO: ADI(G) Report Serial No 234 (Report No 8/106) of 22 April 1944.
2. *Namentliche Verlustmeldung, No 21/44,* Bundesarchiv-Militärarchiv, Freiburg.
3. AIR 40/45, PRO: ADI(G) Report Serial No 234 (Report No 8/106) of 22 April 1944.

4. *British Intelligence in the Second World War, Volume 5 – Strategic Deception*, Michael Howard, London, HMSO, 1990, p. 130. Crown Copyright material is reproduced with the permission of the Controller of HMSO.
5. *Ibid.*
6. AIR 22/500, PRO: RAF Signals Intelligence Air Activity Summary, 18-19 April 1944.
7. Information supplied by Marcel van Heijkop.
8. AIR 25/209, PRO: 11 Group Ops Activity Synopsis – Appendix to Ops Record Book.
9. National Meteorological Archive, Meteorological Office, Bracknell.
10. *Isle of Wight County Press*, 22 April 1944.
11. 50/105, PRO: Personal Combat Report, F/Lt A V Sanders, 266 Squadron.
12. AIR 40/45, PRO: ADI(G) Report Serial No 234 (Report No 8/106) of 22 April 1944.
13. *Ibid.*
14. Information supplied by Marcel van Heijkop.
15. *Beam Benders – 80 Wing RAF*, Laurie Brettingham, Midland Publishing Ltd, 1997, pp. 40-41.
16. *Ibid.*, p. 41.

CHAPTER 9: A Few Loose Ends

1. AIR 50/105, PRO: Personal Combat Report, F/Lt A V Sanders, 266 Squadron.
2. AIR 25/209, PRO: 11 Group Operations Activity Synopsis – Appendix to Ops Record Book.
3. AIR 40/45, PRO: ADI(G) Report Serial No 234 (Report No 8/106) of 22 April 1944.
4. *Second Front – III*, Nevil Shute, Ministry of Information article, 1944.

CHAPTER 10: Reflections

1. *Typhoon Tale*, James Kyle, GM, 1989, p. 152.
2. Memorial Records, Museum of Army Flying.
3. Information from the German War Graves Commission.

ACKNOWLEDGEMENTS

I wish to express my gratitude to the many people who have assisted me with my research. Without their help this book would never have seen the light of day. I apologise in advance if, inadvertently, I have left anyone out of this list of thanks.

First of all, I am extremely grateful to Barry Price for allowing me to refer to the recollections of his late father-in-law, Jock Leal. It was his record of the mysterious events of 18 April 1944 which inspired me to investigate this wartime incident.

Next, my thanks go to all those eyewitnesses whose accounts of the Junkers incident I have been privileged to hear, and who were the real story-tellers in this book:

Firstly, those servicemen and women connected with HMS Mastodon: Ian Gordon, Allan Green, Neil Gregory, George James, Vic Johnson, John Lambourne, Kathleen Maskell, Margaret Mead, Sam Mundy, Maurice Passingham, Vera Selfe, Harry Smelt, Dominica Smith, Professor Richard Stephens, and last, but by no means least, Reg 'Tug' Wilson, who sadly passed away recently.

Also, Peggy Groom, Phyllis Stephens, John Farrell and Ron Woolhead, who were based at RAF Calshot, and Phyllis Lehan-Williams and Yvonne Cooper who served with the Royal Observer Corps at the Operations HQ in Winchester.

Other valued eyewitness contributions were made by David Butler, James Carroll, Margaret Day, Maldwin Drummond, Walter Elsworth, Alan Fields, William Fuller, Nancy Hardy, John Hayward, Honor Johnston, Sylvia Johnston, Marjorie Maidment, Joan McCluskey, John Meredith, Peter Montgomery, Martin Nicholas, Leopold and Rosemary de Rothschild, Arthur Shave, Arthur Sibley and Reg Wheeler.

Maurice Barker gave me the benefit of his considerable local knowledge, and provided very useful information about the crash site and the Prince of Wales's visit to Exbury in 1934. Sadly, Maurice passed away before this book was completed.

For information about the involvement of 266 (Rhodesia) Squadron in this story, I am indebted to the following former Typhoon pilots – Charles Baillie, Geoffrey Henderson (sadly now passed away), Mac McMurdon in Zimbabwe and Ronnie Sheward (CO of 266 Squadron from March to July 1945). I am also grateful to Norma Hughes, widow of Typhoon pilot David Hughes, and to James Kyle, Typhoon pilot of 197 Squadron. In addition, my thanks go to Seymour 'Buck' Feldman of 3 (F) Squadron, Bill Musgrave of 237 Squadron, 'Baron' Humphreys of 613 Squadron, Mr E Jefferies, a fitter with 257 Squadron and Mr E Mole, an armourer with 193 Squadron. Peter Cooke, noted Zimbabwean Air Force historian, sadly passed away during the course of my research. Both he and his wife Anne were most helpful to me.

Next, I must thank two local historians for their help and support. Alan Brown provided very useful information about the Advanced Landing Ground at Needs Oar Point and other wartime airfields in the New Forest. Clare Murley of the Fawley Historians provided details of the burials in the churchyard of All Saints, Fawley, and also helped to solve the puzzle of the missing Iron Cross.

James Toomey gave me valuable information about the anti-aircraft units stationed in the New Forest before D-Day. Richard Myers, Andy Gilliam and Derek Kent also made helpful comments about various aspects of this wartime incident. I am also grateful to John Leete and Patrick Kempe of Flying Films, producers of the film 'The New Forest at War', for the interest they have shown in my research.

Some of my findings were derived from official records, and I should particularly like to thank the following for their assistance: the Air and Navy Historical Branches of the Ministry of Defence, Nicholas Coney at the Public Record Office, Stephen Walton (Archivist) and Alan Wakefield (Curator of the Photographic Archive) at the Imperial War Museum, and Margrit Prussat at the *Deutsches Museum* in Munich. Ian MacGregor of the National Meteorological Archive deserves a special mention for conjuring up surprisingly detailed information about the weather conditions on 18 April 1944. I am grateful to Neville Cullingford and Tony Maasz of the Royal Observer Corps for providing reports and photographs. My thanks also go to Derek Armitage, Archivist at the Museum of Army Flying, for unearthing a record of the Auster crash at Exbury. Andrew

Whitmarsh, Military History Officer, of the Portsmouth Museums and Records Service, was very helpful in providing details of the construction of the Phoenix components of the Mulberry Harbours. The County Reference Library in Newport, Isle of Wight, the libraries at Hythe and Lymington, the Hampshire Record Office in Winchester and the Tourist Information Centre in Shanklin all kindly assisted me in tracking down contemporary press reports and local records.

Further afield, I must thank personnel at the French Air Force base at Avord for information about the Luftwaffe's use of the airfield during the last war. I also received valuable assistance from the German War Graves Commission and the *Deutsche Dienststelle* (WASt) in Berlin. I am grateful to Sebastian Remus and Dr Ekkehart Guth for their research at the *Bundesarchiv-Militärarchiv* in Freiburg on my behalf. Marcel van Heijkop in the Netherlands kindly shared with me his knowledge of KG66 and Soesterberg airfield.

I should like to thank several authors: in particular, Cyril Cunningham for allowing me to use information from his book *The Beaulieu River Goes To War*, Laurie Brettingham for permitting my reference to 'meaconing' from his work *Beam Benders,* James Kyle for letting me quote from his recollections of the Junkers crash in *Typhoon Tale*, and Guy Hartcup for allowing me to use information from his work about the Mulberry harbours. Chris Thomas, author of the *Typhoon and Tempest Story*, made some helpful suggestions about photographs. On the subject of illustrations, I am most grateful to Val Biro for allowing me to reproduce his artwork which graced the dust-jacket of the 1955 Heinemann edition of *Requiem for a Wren*.

Maps are, of course, important in the telling of the Exbury Junkers story. I should like to thank author Cyril Cunningham and Susan Tomkins of Montagu Ventures Ltd for helping me with my search for a contemporary German map of the Solent area, and I am very grateful to Richard Wilson for producing all the remaining maps. My thanks also go to Dan and Janet Gionet for help with IT-related matters.

With regard to the author Nevil Shute's association with the lone German bomber, firstly I must thank several members of the Nevil Shute Norway Foundation for the interest and support they have shown me. Dan Telfair, from Albuquerque, New Mexico, helped me to track down the writer's unpublished Ministry of Information article which explains how his connection with the Exbury Junkers incident came about. Steph Gallagher from Australia kindly accommodated my presentation on the 'Facts behind the Fiction', within a tight day's schedule at Exbury, during the Foundation's UK Conference in June 2003. Richard Michalak, also based in Australia, provided helpful comments and support, and both he and Steph kindly made available several photographs from the day at Exbury. Martyn Dryden also deserves thanks for agreeing to appear in the book. Continuing with the Nevil Shute theme, I am indebted to Professor Julian Smith for allowing me to use background material from his biography of the writer, and to A P Watt Ltd, on behalf of the Trustees of the Estate of the late Nevil Shute Norway, for allowing me to quote from *Requiem for a Wren*.

Much of my analysis of the German bomber's strange behaviour was made possible by the detailed recollections and insights provided by Helmut Thomale, who had also served with 2./KG66 during the *Steinbock* raids. I am very grateful to him for allowing me to refer to his wartime experiences in this book.

My deepest gratitude is expressed to the relatives of four of the seven young men who lost their lives in the Junkers crash: Maria and Hans Otto, Hans Schwingenstein, Karin Oschmann, Ilse Wysotzki and Dr Volker Scholz. I have been very touched by the trust and cooperation which they have afforded me, in providing photographs, copies of letters and other personal information. I sincerely hope that I have not let them down in any way. My special thanks similarly go to Prue Viccars and Chris Reeves - relatives of Captain Hugh Evans, who died in the Auster crash at Exbury on the same day.

The importance of Exbury and the Beaulieu river to the Allied D-Day preparations is central to this book. I should like to offer my heartfelt thanks to all those at Exbury for making me so welcome during my many visits; in particular, Mr Edmund de Rothschild (President of the Exbury Veterans Association [EVA] and owner of Exbury House), Angus Harley (Managing Agent for the Exbury estate), Nigel Philpott (Commercial & Marketing Manager), Jennifer Chaplin (Secretary to Mr Edmund) and Clive Lester (the EVA Chairman). I am also grateful to Mr Nicholas de Rothschild for sparing the time to show me the remains of the anti-aircraft site on the Lower Exbury marshes. My special thanks are reserved for the EVA Secretary, Marion Loveland, and her husband Stuart, for the overwhelming support and kindness which they have shown me over the past seven years.

This has been a long journey, fraught with obstacles and blind alleys, and hampered by the passage of time. But, among other things, it has given me the opportunity to blow away the cobwebs from my education in French and German languages. On the latter point, I should like to thank Marion Pollard for helping me greatly with my German translation, and for giving me less red ink at the end than when I first embarked on this quest.

Finally, to my wife Julie, and children Adam and Jennifer, for tolerating my obsession. Thank you.

LIST OF ILLUSTRATIONS

Photographs

The author wishes to thank the following for providing the photographs reproduced in this book (listed by illustration number):

3.	EN Archive.
4.	Royal Observer Corps Museum, Winchester.
5.	No 14 Group, the Royal Observer Corps Association.
6.	EN Archive.
7.	Sam Mundy.
9.	Imperial War Museum (CH 11583).
10.	Joan McCluskey and Marjorie Maidment.
12.	Harry Smelt.
13.	John Lambourne.
14.	Wendy Edwards.
15.	Neil Gregory.
16.	Sam Mundy.
17-18.	Allan Green.
19.	Richard Stephens.
20.	Maurice Barker.
21.	Nancy Hardy.
22-24.	Phyllis Stephens.
25.	Museum of Army Flying.
26-27.	Maria and Hans Otto.
29.	Barry Price.
30.	Ilse Wysotzki.
31-33.	Karin Oschmann.
34-36.	Maria and Hans Otto.
37.	Dr Volker Scholz.
38.	Karin Oschmann.
39.	Imperial War Museum (MH 7518).

40. Helmut Thomale.
41. Ilse Wysotzki.
42. EN Archive.
43. Barry Price.
44-45. EN Archive.
46. Helmut Thomale.
47-48. EN Archive.
52. Imperial War Museum (A 24165).
53. Imperial War Museum (CH 13236).
54. Imperial War Museum (CH 18770).
58. Imperial War Museum (A 23276).
61-62. The Nevil Shute Norway Foundation.
63. Imperial War Museum (CH 15683).
64. The Exbury Veterans Association.
68. Imperial War Museum (CH 13238).
69. Deutsches Museum (R2643-4).
70. Deutsches Museum (R1079-2).
71. Ronnie Sheward.
79. Edmund de Rothschild/Paul Cave Publications Ltd (original taken by Mudge of Fawley).
80-81. Honor Johnston (originals taken by Mudge of Fawley).
82. James Kyle.
83. Nancy Hardy.
84. Joan McCluskey.
85. Maurice Barker.
93. Hans Schwingenstein.

All other photographs were taken by the author.

Maps

The author is grateful to the following:

- Lord Montagu of Beaulieu for permitting the German map of the Solent area (illustration 1) to be reproduced and annotated;
- Richard Wilson for producing illustrations 2, 11, 55 and 65. (Illustration 55 based on an original by Alan Brown.)

Miscellaneous

The following additional sources are gratefully acknowledged:

28. Public Record Office (AIR50/105).
60. Original artwork by Val Biro.
66. Isle of Wight County Press.
67. Lymington Times.
86. Karin Oschmann.

BIBLIOGRAPHY

Published works

Air War over the Isle of Wight, H J T Leal, Isle of Wight County Press, 1982.

Battles in the Skies over the Isle of Wight, H J T Leal, Isle of Wight County Press, 1988, reprinted 1993.

Beam Benders – 80 Wing RAF, Laurie Brettingham, Midland Publishing Ltd, 1997.

The Beaulieu River Goes To War, Cyril Cunningham, Montagu Ventures Ltd, 1994.

Blitz on Britain, Alfred Price, Sutton Publishing Ltd, 2000.

The Blitz, Then and Now, Volume 3, Battle of Britain Prints International Ltd, 1990.

British Intelligence in the Second World War, Volume 5 – Strategic Deception, Michael Howard, London, HMSO, 1990.

Code Name Mulberry: The Planning, Building and Operation of the Normandy Harbours, Guy Hartcup, David & Charles, 1977.

Nevil Shute, Julian Smith, Twayne Publishers, 1976, reprinted by the Paper Tiger, Cresskill, NJ, 2002.

Our Exbury, A. J. Holland & Edmund de Rothschild, Paul Cave Publications Ltd, 1982.

Requiem for a Wren, Nevil Shute, William Heinemann Ltd, 1955.

Twelve Airfields, Alan Brown, 1997.

Typhoon Tale, James Kyle, GM, 1989.

Unpublished works

HMS Mastodon – A Short History, Cyril Cunningham, 1992.

Second Front – III, Nevil Shute, Ministry of Information article, 1944.

Official Records

Public Record Office:

AIR 16/173: Anti-Aircraft Operations against Enemy Aircraft, 18 April 1944.

AIR 16/962: Combats and Casualties Report, 18 April 1944.

AIR 22/500: RAF Signals Intelligence Air Activity Summary, 18/19 April 1944.

AIR 25/209: 11 Group Ops Activity Synopsis – Appendix to Ops Record Book.

AIR 27/1559: Ops Record, 266 Squadron.

AIR 40/45: ADI(G) Report Serial No 234 (Report No 8/106), 22 April 1944.

AIR 40/173: The Junkers 188.

AIR 40/1166: Air Technical Intelligence Items.

AIR 40/2417: ADI(K) Report No 170/1944, 19 April 1944.

AIR 50/105: Personal Combat Report, F/Lt A V Sanders, 266 Squadron.

Bundesarchiv:

I/KG66, Einsatz England, Hans Hebestreit, RL 10/638.

Einsatz gegen England 1943-1944, RL 8/65.

Extract from *Verlustfilm 96/10.*

Extract from *Bordfilm 139/20.*

Extract from *Bordfilm 150/52.*

Extract from *Bordfilm 163/93.*

Extract from *Bordfilm 169/108.*

Kampfgeschwader 6, RL 10/564.

Namentliche Verlustliste, Kampfgeschwader 26, 1939-1945, O IV 72.

Namentliche Verlustmeldung, No 21/44.

Verluste I/KG66, RL 10/638.

Wehrstammbuch of *Obergefreiter* Hans Ehrhardt.

Wehrstammbuch and *Wehrpaß* of *Gefreiter* Edgar Vester.

Miscellaneous

German War Graves Commission leaflet.

Isle of Wight County Press, 22 April 1944.

Memorial Records, Museum of Army Flying.

National Meteorological Archive, Meteorological Office, Bracknell.

New Milton and District Advertiser & Lymington Times, 22 April 1944.

Operations Log No 70 of 3 Group ROC, 18 April 1944.

INDEX

Air Ministry
  Air Ministry investigation 32, 75, 81;
  Air Ministry official 98
Air raid siren(s) 2, 4
Ambulance
  ambulance driver 22, 28-9;
  field ambulance, HMS Mastodon 22;
  Morris 14 ambulance 28;
  transportation of bodies to RAF Calshot 28-9
Auster, light observation plane
  crash at Exbury 29-30, 97, 98;
  role in support of ground troops 29, 98
Austria
  Grafenbach 37;
  Vienna 37

Barker, Maurice 25, 99
Barker, Mrs 99
Beaulieu
  Beaulieu river xi,, xv, 7, 34, 58, 60, 61, 63, 67, 69, 74, 75, 84, 89;
  The Beaulieu River Goes To War (Cyril Cunningham) 60, 67;
  Land Army Girls' hostel 11, 30, 97
Belgian Browning 99
Belgium
  Antwerp 79;
  Brussels 47, 83, 85;
  Chièvres 38, 50
Biro, Val, artist and children's author 69
Blackfield Baptist chapel 99
Bombing
  Allied bombing of German cities 53, 54, 57, 58;
  Luftwaffe raids on Britain, 1943 50;
  see also Steinbock ('little blitz')
British air defences
  356 Heavy Anti-Aircraft Battery 63;
  Anti-Aircraft Command 32, 71;
  anti-aircraft defences, Needs Oar Point 63;
  anti-aircraft fire 4, 5, 6, 7, 9, 11, 13, 17, 32, 68, 71, 81, 85;
  anti-aircraft gunners/crews/sites 6, 26, 32, 81, 86, 87, 89;
  Anti-Aircraft Operations against Enemy Aircraft (report) 32;
  anti-aircraft site, Lepe Farm 11, 13;
  anti-aircraft site, Lower Exbury 7, 32, 88-9;
  anti-aircraft site, Lynn Farm, Isle of Wight 5;
  Bofors gun(s) 4, 7, 32, 68, 89;
  night fighters 51;
  Oerlikon gun(s) 69, 70;
  protection for invasion force, New Forest 63;
  radar 1, 79;
  Vickers gun(s) 6
British intelligence officers 45, 53
Brown, Alan 64
Butler, David 26-7

Cadland House 10
Calshot 8, 10;
  see also Royal Air Force, RAF Calshot
Cannock Chase, German Military Cemetery 100-101
Carroll, James 4
Cassino, Battle of xi
Combined Operations
  Combined Operations Bombardment Unit 16, 19, 71;
  commissioning of HMS Mastodon 59;
  preparations for D-Day 58
Cooper, Bunty 11;
  see also Joan McCluskey
Crash site
  casualties 19-21, 22, 23, 25, 26, 28-9, 46;
  civilians 21, 26-7, 71;
  copse 26, 28, 75, 94;
  documents found 27, 32, 34;
  engines 17, 18, 21-2, 25-6, 71, 91, 92;
  finds by a metal detector 93;
  French coins 26;
  identity discs 34, 36, 44, 72;
  live ammunition 20, 26, 27, 81;
  maps 44-5, 53;
  personal belongings 26;
  police sergeant 26;
  pond 17, 20, 21, 26, 75, 91, 92, 93, 94;

RAF inspection 27, 32, 67, 72, 90;
removal of the bodies 28-9;
sixty years on 91, 106;
taking of souvenirs 26, 27, 44, 99;
visit by anti-aircraft crew and Typhoon pilots 26, 95;
wreckage 19, 20, 21, 26, 27, 29, 32, 44, 46, 53, 67, 75, 81, 92, 98
Crete 37, 44
Cunningham, Cyril, author of *The Beaulieu River Goes To War* 60, 67
Czech Republic
Sternberk (formerly Sternberg) 37;
see also Sudetenland
Czipin, Johann (Hans), *Unteroffizier* 37, 38, 43, 47, 102

Daniels, Albert, Sick Berth CPO, HMS Mastodon 21
Day, Margaret 30
D-Day
50th Anniversary, 1994 93;
Allied invasion preparations xv, 7, 16, 34, 47, 58-65, 67, 74, 82, 87, 107;
Force J, Assault Group 1 15, 22;
Gold, Juno, Sword sectors 58, 59;
Mulberry Harbours 60-61;
Normandy landings 47, 58, 60, 61, 67, 74, 76, 87, 95, 106;
Omaha Beach 106;
Operation Fortitude 65, 76;
Phoenixes, construction of 60-61;
sensitive Allied military installations 58-65, 75, 86, 107
Defection
defection theory 34, 74, 77-82;
fictional account in *Requiem for a Wren* 69, 71-2
De Havilland Dragon, King's Flight 93-5;
Denmark 42
Dodd, Donovan, F/Sgt, 266 Squadron 10-11, 62, 80, 98
Dornier Do 217 51, 56, 84
Drummond, Maldwin 10
Dryden, Martyn 73
Dudley, Mary, Second Officer, WRNS, HMS Mastodon 24
Dungeness 61

East Hill Farm 11
Ehrhardt, Hans, *Obergefreiter* 38-9, 43, 47, 100, 102
English Channel 1, 74, 77, 78, 79, 84, 89
Evans, Hugh, Capt, Royal Artillery 98
Exbury
Exbury estate 9, 15, 17, 60, 75, 81, 100, 104;
Exbury Gardens 104, 105;
'Exbury Hall' (*Requiem for a Wren*) 73;
Exbury House xi , 7-8, 12, 15-16, 17, 22, 23, 24, 58-9, 60, 73, 91, 93, 105;
see also HMS Mastodon *and* Rothschild family;
Exbury Veterans Association 104, 105;
Exbury village 11, 12, 13, 17, 25, 27, 29, 85, 104;
Lower Exbury 7, 32, 88-9;
Lower Exbury road 13, 17, 19, 22, 28, 68, 75, 91, 94;
Marise Cottage 12;
'The Park' 17;
planting of commemorative oak 104;
Remembrance Sunday 104;
St Katharine's Parish Church 104;
water tower 8, 9, 15

Fawley
All Saints Church 30-31, 101;
burial of the German airmen 30-31, 96, 100;
German graves 39, 95, 100;
visit by German relative (c.1958) 99
Fields, Alan 13
France
Arromanches 61;
Avord airfield 1, 36, 42, 44-5, 53-4, 56, 57, 77-8, 83, 84;
Bourges 1, 53;
Brest peninsula 84;
Brétigny 37, 38, 44;
Brittany 76, 84;
Chartres 50;
Laon 55, 57;
Le Havre 1-2, 79;
Montdidier 42, 43, 51, 52, 55, 56;
Normandy 47, 58, 60, 61, 67, 74, 76, 87, 95, 98, 106;
Paimpol 84;
Paris 44, 53;
Pas de Calais 65, 76

Fuller, William 6

'Gee' navigation system;
see KG66
Geneva 53
German High Command 65
German Military Cemetery, Cannock Chase 100-102
German Reich 36
German War Graves Commission 100
Germany
Augsburg 39;
Augsburg, Rudolf Diesel Engineering School 39;
Berlin 54;
Crailsheim 38;
Dortmund 37, 41;
Flensburg 42;
Friedrichshafen-Bodensee, Dornier works 40;
Goslar 41;
Ilmenau 38;
Jüterbog 37;
Köthen 53;
Leipzig 42;
National Work Service 39;
Werl 41
Gordon, Ian, Assault Group 1, Force J 22
Göring, Hermann, *Reichsmarschall*, C-in-C Luftwaffe 54-5, 57;
see also Steinbock ('little blitz')
Green, Allan, Sick Berth Attendant, HMS Mastodon 22-3
Gregory, Neil, Combined Operations Bombardment Unit 19, 20

Hampshire
coast 7, 30, 34, 47, 54, 60, 74, 78, 84;
mainland xiii, 32, 58, 77, 85, 86
Hardy, Nancy (née Jones) 97;
see also Nancy Jones
Hawker Typhoon Mk 1B;
see Typhoons
Hayward, John 6
Heinkel He 177 56
Hellier, Phyllis, WAAF ambulance driver 28-9
Hern, Kathleen, Wren 25
Hitler, Adolf 38, 54
Hitler Youth organisation 38, 40, 41
HMS Mastodon
commissioned 7, 59;
dentist 15, 21, 22, 23-4;
despatch rider 7, 15, 19, 21;
fire-crew 15;
guardhouse 59;
medical officer 21;
Nissen hut(s) 7, 15, 16, 19, 23, 25, 60;
parade-ground 5;
paymaster 24;
perimeter 19;
planning and preparations for D-Day xi, 7, 59-60;
sick bay 21, 22-3, 25, 96;
Sick Berth Attendant 22-3;
Sick Berth CPO 21;
signals training 16;
Transport Section 21;
Wren(s) 22, 24, 25, 60, 68, 69, 71, 92, 96;
see also Exbury House, Combined Operations *and* D-Day
HMS Vectis, Royal Yacht Squadron, Cowes 58
HMS Vernon, Portsmouth 15
Holbury 17
Home Guard 5
Huggins, Godfrey, Hon., Prime Minister, Southern Rhodesia 62, 80
Hughes, David, DFC, F/Lt, 266 Squadron 87

Identities of the seven men xiv, 34, 36-43, 47, 72, 77
Ilfracombe 84
Iron Cross medal 26, 41, 44, 99
Isle of Wight
Cowes 4, 58;
Cowes Roads 4;
Duxmore Farm 5;
East Cowes 4, 5, 6;
Gurnard 6;
Isle of Wight County Press 79;
Ju 188 flight over the island xvi, 1-6, 18, 34, 58, 70, 75, 79-80, 81, 84-5, 87;
Little Thorness Farm 6;
Lynn Farm 5;
Mount Joy 3, 6;
The Needles 3;
Newport 3, 4, 6;
Newtown 3;
Parkhurst forest 4;
river Medina 4;

Ryde 4;

St Catherine's Point 2, 3, 78;
Sandown 4;
Somerton Aerodrome 4;
Thorness Bay 6;
West Cowes 4, 80

James, George, Combined Operations Bombardment Unit 16, 19, 20, 21, 71
Jamming 51, 52
Johnston, Honor 11
Johnston, Sylvia 13
Jones, Nancy 11, 27, 30;
see also Nancy Hardy
Junkers
Junkers Ju 52 55;
Junkers Ju 88 25, 48, 50, 51, 56;
test flights 42;
Junkers Ju 188
BMW-801 radial engines 25, 48;
camouflage 33;
cockpit 10, 13, 16, 17, 19, 34, 36, 46-7, 48-49, 71-2, 77, 80, 85;
compass 56, 84, 86, 90;
crew positions 46-7;
direction-finding and homing equipment 89-90;
distinguishing features 5, 48-50;
identification/side markings 32-3, 36, 43, 47, 56;
interrogation of a Ju 188 pilot 32, 45;
Ju 188 A, D variants 48;
Ju 188 E variant 48, 52, 74;
Jumo engines 48;
Long Wave radio 89-90;
lowering of undercarriage 70, 82;
Luftwaffe report into loss of Ju 188 Z6 EK 76, 100;
parachute(s) 13, 21, 71, 85;
performance and comparison with Ju 88 46, 48, 50;
production and introduction to service 48, 50;
roles 48;
transportation of ground crew 44-5, 46;
transportation of secret agents 46;
Z6 EK, black underside 6, 11, 33, 70, 76;
Z6 EK, crash at Exbury 17-18, 67, 71;
Z6 EK, crew ages 42;
Z6 EK, crew numbers xi, xiii, 20-21, 26, 34, 36, 43-7, 68, 69, 71-2, 74, 77;
Z6 EK, crew ranks 42-3, 72;
Z6 EK, crew service records 36, 44;
Z6 EK, deviation from intended course 44-5, 47, 77-80, 82-5, 86, 89-90;
see also KG66 and *Steinbock* ('little blitz')

KG66, specialist pathfinder unit
I/KG66 50-51, 52, 53, 54, 55, 56, 57, 76, 77, 82, 83;
2./KG66 32-3, 36, 37, 38, 39, 40, 42-3, 44, 45, 46, 47, 51, 53, 55, 76, 78, 84, 90;
aircraft types used 51;
bases used 50, 51, 53;
conversion from Ju 88 to Ju 188 51;
direction-finding and homing equipment 56, 89-90;
Düppel tin foil (cf. RAF's use of 'Window') 51;
Egon (cf. RAF 'Oboe') navigation system 52;
'Gee' (*Truhe*) navigation system 47, 52-3;
ground crew 36, 39-42, 44, 45, 46, 53, 56, 57, 78, 82-3;
morale in I/KG66 82;
navigation 45, 47, 51, 52, 53, 56, 82-6, 89-90;
pathfinding and target-marking 48, 50-52, 56, 76, 78;
support to *IX Fliegerkorps* 50, 55;
tactics 51-2;
X and Y radio navigation systems 51;
see also Junkers Ju 188 *and* Steinbock ('little blitz')
Krause, Johann, *Unteroffizier* 37, 38, 43, 44, 47, 102
Kyle, James, DFM, F/Lt, 197 Squadron 26, 95-6

Lambourne, John, Marine 16-17, 19-20, 106
Land (Army) Girls 11-12, 27, 29-30, 96-7
Landing craft
build-up in the Solent and Beaulieu river 7, 58, 60, 65, 74, 77;
Landing Craft Support 16;
tank landing craft (LCT) 67, 68, 69, 70
Leal, Jock, L/Observer, Royal Observer Corps xiii, 3, 18, 34-5, 81
Lee-on-Solent 7

Lehan, Phyllis, Royal Observer Corps 2-3, 20
Lepe
Lepe Beach 60-61;
Lepe Farm 11, 13;
Lepe House 17, 25
Lincoln 50
London, Luftwaffe raids 44, 50, 56, 78
Lord, Walter, Lt-Cdr, paymaster, HMS Mastodon 24
Luftwaffe, crew members
1. Wart (Chief Ground Crew) 40;
Beobachter (lit. 'observer', cf. RAF navigator) 37, 43, 44, 46, 47, 56, 81, 84-5, 90;
Bordfunker (radio operator) 37, 41, 42, 43, 45, 46, 47, 53, 56, 81, 84, 86, 90;
Bordschütze (air gunner) 19, 38, 43, 46, 47;
Flugzeugführer (pilot) 3, 16, 32, 34, 37, 43, 45, 46, 47, 53, 56, 79, 82, 83, 84-5, 89, 93, 95;
Funkwart (radio technician) 41, 42, 45, 56
Luftwaffe, formations
(*see also KG66*, specialist pathfinder unit);
IX Fliegerkorps 50, 55, 57;
Erprobungs Kommando 188 50;
KG2 55;
KG6 37, 38, 43, 44, 50, 55;
KG26 37;
Legion Condor, Spanish Civil War 38;
Luftflotte 3 55, 57
Luftwaffe, miscellaneous
air intelligence 41, 42, 76;
anticipation of Allied invasion 56-7;
badge/insignia 28, 29, 47;
landings in Britain 83-4;
ranks, RAF equivalents 42, 72;
uniform(s) 19, 22, 28, 29

McCluskey, Joan (née Cooper) 97;
see also Bunty Cooper
McMurdon, Mac, 266 Squadron 7, 26, 98
Maidment, Marjorie (née Pinnock) 97;
see also Marjorie Pinnock
Mead, Margaret, Wren 92-3
Merchant Navy 4
Meredith, John 5
Messerschmitts
Me 109s 55;
Me 410s 56
Montgomery, Peter 4
Mundy, Sam, despatch rider, HMS Mastodon 7-8, 15, 19, 21-2

Nazi regime 34, 71, 74
Needs Oar Point
Advanced Landing Ground xv, 7, 9, 26, 29, 61-4, 86, 87;
plaque marking site of ALG 64;
visit by Prime Minster of Southern Rhodesia 62, 80
New Forest 63, 64
New Milton and District Advertiser & Lymington Times 79
North Sea 56
Nottingham 11, 29

Passingham, Maurice 81
Peltz, Dietrich, *Oberst*, Commander, *IX Fliegerkorps* 50, 51
Pinnock, Marjorie 11;
see also Marjorie Maidment
Poland
Nowe Guty (formerly Seegutten) 38;
Toruń (formerly Thorn) 40;
Wolin (formerly Wollin, Pomerania) 42
Polish destroyer 5
Prince of Wales, Edward, visit to Exbury, May 1934 93-5
Princess Margaret (ship) 4
Pugsley, A., Captain, Commander Assault Group 1, Force J 22

Reconnaissance
aerial photograph of Beaulieu river area 75;
Air reconnaissance of Allied invasion fleet 76;
Photo-reconnaissance theory about Exbury Junkers 34, 70, 74, 75-7
Rhodesia 7, 61, 62, 80, 87, 98
Rothschild family
Edmund xi, 104;
Leopold 12;
Mrs Lionel 94;
owners of Exbury House 58, 59, 105;
Prince of Wales's visit in 1934 93;
Rosemary 12;
see also Exbury House *and* HMS Mastodon
Royal Air Force (RAF)
11 Group 2;
80 (Signals) Wing 83;

146 Wing, 84 Group, 2nd Tactical Air Force 61-2;
197 Squadron 26, 32, 95, 96;
266 (Rhodesia) Squadron 7, 9, 11, 14, 26, 32, 61-2, 80, 86, 87, 95, 98;
313 Squadron 32;
439 Squadron 32;
661 Squadron 98;
Air Observation Post Squadrons 98;
Exercise Smash 7, 9;
intelligence officer(s) 70, 72; 76;
'meaconing' 83-84;
RAF Calshot 8-9, 28, 30;
RAF Signals Intelligence Air Activity Summary 77
Royal Marine(s) 4, 16, 19, 22, 60, 106
Royal Navy
Exbury House commandeered 7, 58-9;
Women's Royal Naval Service (WRNS), Wrens 22, 24, 25, 60, 68, 69, 71, 92, 96;
see also Combined Operations *and* HMS Mastodon
Royal Observer Corps (ROC)
3 Group HQ, Winchester 2, 20, 86;
German aircraft recognition book 50;
observer post, Mount Joy, Newport xiii, 2, 3, 6, 18, 34, 81;
ROC alarm 2
Runstedt, Gerd von, *Generalfeldmarschall*, Commander Western Front 76-7

Sanders, Vernon, DFC, F/Lt, 266 Squadron
intercept of the Junkers 7, 9-11, 17, 80, 98;
Personal Combat Report 10, 17, 33, 80, 81, 86
Schultes, Robert, *Unteroffizier* 37, 38, 43, 47, 102
Schwingenstein, Hans 103
Schwingenstein, Leonhard, *Obergefreiter* 39-41, 44, 45, 53, 57, 58, 78, 82-3, 103
Seegutten, East Prussia (Nowe Guty in today's Poland) 38
Selsey 61
Shave, George 4
Sheward, Ronnie, DFC, S/Ldr, 266 Squadron 87
Shute, Nevil , novelist
Blind Understanding 66, 68-9;
comparison of fictional account with Junkers incident xiv-xv, 70-72;
connections with HMS Mastodon and Beaulieu river xi, 67;
Lt-Cdr Nevil Shute Norway, RNVR 66-7;
Nevil Shute Norway Foundation, visit to Exbury in 2003 73;
Requiem for a Wren xi, xiv-xv, 34, 46, 66, 69-72,73, 82;
Second Front – III, Ministry of Information article 67-8, 71, 90;
speculation about the Exbury Junkers mystery 67-8, 90;
war correspondent, Ministry of Information 67, 71
Sibley, Arthur 17
Slavonic names/origins 34, 36, 72, 77
Slavs 34, 69, 72
Smelt, Harry, RN stoker, HMS Mastodon fire-crew 15
Soesterberg, Holland 44-5, 46, 56, 78, 79, 82, 83, 84, 85, 89
Solent xi, 4, 6, 7, 34, 58, 60, 61, 63, 64, 70, 74, 87
South Africa 98
Southampton
evacuee from 13;
Southampton Water 8, 84;
Supermarine Works 25
Spanish Civil War 38
Sperrle, Hugo, Generalfeldmarschall, C-in-C Luftflotte 3 55, 56-7
Spitfire(s) 25, 32
Stansore Point, construction of Phoenixes 60, 61
Steinbock, ('little blitz')
bomber force 55, 56;
briefing of *IX Fliegerkorps* crews 55;
cost to Luftwaffe 55-6;
pathfinding and target-marking 56, 76, 78;
planning 54-5;
raids on Britain 54, 56, 58, 78;
use of advanced airfields 45, 46, 55, 56, 78;
see also KG66 and Junkers Ju 188
Stephens, Richard, Surgeon Lt (D), RNVR, HMS Mastodon 15-16, 21, 22, 23, 24
Sternberg (Sternberk in today's Czech Republic) 37;
Sudetenland 36, 37

Taylorcraft Auster Mk 4;
see Auster, light observation plane

Templecombe 84
Thomale, Helmut 45, 46-7, 53, 56, 81, 82, 84, 86, 89, 90, 106
Typhoons 7, 9-11, 12-13, 14, 15, 16, 17, 18, 26, 29, 32, 33, 61-2, 68, 71, 80, 81, 85, 86, 93, 98;
see also Royal Air Force, 266 Squadron *and* Needs Oar Point

Vardy, Mr 11, 12
Very lights
firing of red Very lights xiii; 3, 6, 7, 10, 18, 34, 77, 80, 81, 85;
Luftwaffe use of coloured flares as a deception measure 81;
red signal cartridges 81-2;
Very pistol 81
Vester, Edgar, *Gefreiter* 41-42, 44, 56, 58, 102

Weather conditions 1, 7, 56, 70, 79, 82-3, 84, 89
Wheeler, Reg 99
Wilson, Reg 'Tug', Leading Seaman, HMS Mastodon 17-18, 91
Winchester 2, 20, 86
Wollin, Pomerania (Wolin in today's Poland) 42
Women's Royal Naval Service (WRNS), Wrens;
see Royal Navy
Woolhead, Ron, RAF Calshot 8, 30
Wysotzki, Eitel, *Unteroffizier* 38, 43, 47, 102

Zimbabwe 98